To Sarge,

"facts matter."

Jerry Anderson

www.thepeacemakers.co

Troy, Alabama

11/22/14

Where are the
PEACEMAKERS?

Commentaries About Peace and War

Jerry Henderson

authorHOUSE®

AuthorHouse™
1663 Liberty Drive
Bloomington, IN 47403
www.authorhouse.com
Phone: 1-800-839-8640

Published by AuthorHouse   08/14/2012

ISBN: 978-1-4685-8708-1 (sc)
ISBN: 978-1-4685-8706-7 (hc)
ISBN: 978-1-4685-8707-4 (e)

Library of Congress Control Number: 2012907202

Proceeds from the sale of this book will go to support various grassroots and community based peace, women, children, internally displaced people, and person with disabilities organizations, many of the organizations are listed with details, in this book.

Jerry Henderson
jerryhenderson@thepeacemakers.co
www.thepeacemakers.co

DEDICATION

This book is dedicated to the children of the world. Children are precious, innocent, and vulnerable. They are the primary victims of man-made poverty, war, violence, and destruction.

Blessed are the peacemakers for they shall be called children of God.

Matthew 5:9

CONTENTS

What about the Children?

PREFACE

In late 2002 and early 2003, the world was focused on the United States of America and Iraq. At the time, there was much talk and actions regarding the possibility of a United States led invasion of Iraq. The 'rationale' for such a potential invasion was to locate and expose Iraq's 'weapons of mass destruction.' The allegations charged that Iraq was engaged in the manufacturing and stockpiling of 'weapons of mass destruction.'

At the time, I begin to write about the 'politics of war'—attempting to place the issues of peace, war, global security, and stability into perspective. Then, the world was volatile and insecure. Today, the world is even more volatile and more insecure. This reality exists because certain leaders of nations are engaged in irresponsible actions, and, at the same time, they are in a state of denial about certain truths. What are some of those truths? 1) This is God's world, 2) We are all children of God, 3) The ultimate security of this world is linked to love and justice not war, and 4) "Wisdom is better than weapons of war." The world's volatile and insecure reality is caused by a complex combination of forces at play as nations, individuals, and organizations define the world from their own narrow perspectives: power and power struggles, greed, corruption, the quest for strategic and logistical advantages (land), oil, and other natural resources. As a result of having fundamental differences—nations, individuals, and organizations are waging struggles—including armed struggles—based on their beliefs and differences.

The United States of America, Great Britain, Afghanistan, Iraq, Iran, Uganda, Sudan, North Korea, and the Middle East reflect these differences in public policies and actions. Unfortunately, there are violent, bloody, deadly, and destructive realities. Reflecting on these realities, this book, *Where Are The Peacemakers?* is a collection of 31 commentaries and essays. The commentaries and essays are designed to *inform, stimulate discussions and debates, educate,* and *encourage* more involvement by God's people—a broader involvement in the much needed dialogue, a broader involvement for positive action. As Ban Ki-Moon, Secretary General of the United Nations (UN) stated, "If we do not deal with the root causes of conflict—and offer sustainable solutions—we will be left with humanitarian emergencies and peacekeeping operations without end." There is a critical need for peacemakers. Just as Esther, a biblical child of God said, 'for such a time as this.'

JH

November 2008

A PERSPECTIVE

It gives me great pleasure to have this rare opportunity to associate with Jerry Henderson's book, Where are the Peacemakers? Peace is a God-given gift to mankind. In the New Testament of the Bible, when Jesus appeared to the Apostles after his resurrection, he greeted them *"peace be with you,"* John 20:19. Muslims in particular greet one another, "As-Salamu Alaikum" ('peace be upon you'). In response, Wa'alaikum Salam (peace of Allah/God be with you).

Mankind has destroyed peace because of greed for material possessions and thirst for power. Consequently, there are civil unrest and war everywhere in the world. Within individuals, it is manifested through suicides, in families, it is manifested through domestic violence, and within nations, it is manifested through insurgency and civil strife. Nations fight against nations. All states have experienced war in their history in one way or another.

Governments and people live in perpetual fear. Consequently, large sums of money which would be used for development is diverted to purchase weapons of destruction. The people who are most affected in these wars are innocent men, women, children, and persons with disabilities. In developing poor countries, poverty levels are increasing. People depend on relief aid to survive. Something must be done to reverse such situation. Towards this end, it is important to document and disseminate information about wars, causes, effects, and solutions.

Jerry Henderson is one person who has dedicated his life working in war-ravaged areas, especially in Africa. He has accumulated a wealth of information on the effects of war and the need for peace, thus writing the book, Where are the Peacemakers? *I would like to encourage other peacemakers around the world to study this book and to use it as a tool and reference material in lobbying to bring about peace.*

I wish to thank Jerry for writing a series of books and other publications and also giving me the opportunity to appear in this book.

May God reward him abundantly!

Honorable Baba Diri Margaret
Woman Member of Parliament
Parliament of Uganda
Koboko District
Uganda, East Africa

INTRODUCTION

Where Are The Peacemakers? is a collection of 31 commentaries and essays—each focused on a specific and particular violent, bloody, deadly, and destructive conflict and or potential conflict. This book provides both description and prescription (anyone can criticize). The focus is on places, actions, inactions, dates, and participants: countries, individuals, and organizations. Three of the commentaries focus particularly on children—their plights in wars, conflicts, destruction, poverty, and chaos around the world. Expressions, poetry, and drawings are provided from children in the United States, Uganda, and the Republic of Serpska—three countries, three continents. A section titled Organizations (with contacts) is provided for and to you—the reader. Hopefully, you can and will use the information and help reach out and make a positive contribution and difference—especially for the children. The children of the world need more protection, love, care, and advocates. You can help make a difference.

CHAPTER 1

Five Decades of Conflicts and Wars: The World Says No to the Invasion of Iraq—March 7, 2003

As conflict, turmoil, war, and the threats of more conflict, more turmoil, more wars, and more threats of wars prevail in almost fifty (50) countries—internal conflicts and conflicts between nations—the question should be raised—facts and analysis provided relative to the fundamental question. The fundamental question is where are the peacemakers?

What has been offered as a substitute for peacemakers is *peacekeepers*. While offering peacekeepers and international peacekeeping missions may be well intended, the reality is—one cannot keep the peace which has not been made. Simply stated, the peace must first be made before any realistic efforts can be made to keep the peace. So, we are moving with step 2 before putting step 1 into place. This approach may very well bring about 'short term fixes,' but it will not provide for 'long term solutions.'

If one would realistically look at what I call 50-50-50, the seriousness of the situation becomes much clearer. The 50-50-50 numbers refer to at least 50 major conflicts and wars in 50 different countries—in the past 50 years (and some are still ongoing today).

During this same period, the Nobel Peace Prize has been awarded to individuals who have worked for global peace. Two such individuals are Nelson Mandela, former President of South African, and Desmond Tutu, former Archbishop of Cape Town, South Africa and chairman of South Africa's Truth and Reconciliation Commission (the Commission, which was appointed by President Mandela, held public hearings and conducted investigations into political, economic, and violent crimes which were committed during the unjust and inhumane system of apartheid which ruled South Africa for decades). Mandela, then and now, continues to be a moral leader of the world as he speaks out and pushes for global peace—in a non-compromising style. In fact, and even somewhat surprising, Shimeon Peres, Israeli Foreign Minister, was quoted at the Earth Summit in Johannesburg, South Africa, a few years ago as saying, "If we had Nelson Mandela in the Middle East, we would have peace."

Kofi Annan, Secretary General of the United Nations has led the world body *in, around,* and *through* conflicts, turmoil, and wars throughout the world—many times providing wisdom and genuine leadership on one hand (even when/though some do not want to listen), and providing 'peacekeeping missions' on the other hand—while the wait continues for the peace which has yet to be made. Where are the peacemakers?

An examination of the record reveals that during the past fifty (50) years, the world has witnessed conflicts, turmoil, wars, and the threats of wars in and between many countries:

Afghanistan	Ghana	Namibia
Algeria	Guyana	Nigeria
Angola	Guatemala	Nicaragua
Albania	Haiti	Panama
Bosnia & Herzegovina	Israel	Pakistan
Bolivia	Indonesia	Philippines
Burma	India	Rwanda
Burundi	Iran	Sierra Leone
Columbia	Iraq	Somalia

China	Ivory Coast	Sri Lanka
Democratic Republic of the Congo (DRC)	Jamaica	Sudan
East Timor	Kosovo	South Africa
El Salvador	Lebanon	Thailand
Ethiopia	Malaysia	Taiwan
Eritrea	Mexico	Uganda
Former Soviet Union (Russia)		Venezuela
		Yugoslavia
		Zimbabwe

Conflict and wars do not just happen out of the blue. For the most part, there are four (4) primary factors at the heart of all conflicts and wars:

1. **Power and power struggles**: the desire to be in control. The desire to rule.

2. **Greed**: the desire to obtain as much as can be obtained.

3. **Corruption**: stealing and taking that which belongs to another/others (money, minerals, and other natural resources).

4. **Strategic and logistics (land, air, and sea)**: global military locations and other advantages.

Where are the peacemakers, where is the peace, where is justice, where are the genuine leaders, where is the moral leadership?

During the past few years in particular, much has been said about "terrorism" and "weapons of mass destruction." Terrorism and weapons of mass destruction should be part of a robust dialogue—national and international. The issues and facts concerning weapons of mass destruction should be put on the table for discussion, analysis, clarity, and understanding. These terms and concepts should be qualified and operational definitions applied to both. We must avoid the flaw of having someone politically decide and define for each of us, who is a terrorist and who has weapons of mass destruction. The issues should be carefully examined and clearly articulated. Unfortunately, there is a refusal on the part of the leadership in Washington to debate the facts of the matter. People are told, we are preparing to go to Iraq. Where is the debate?

Other issues and concerns should also be raised: What are weapons of mass destruction? Who determines whether a weapon is a weapon of mass destruction?—by what authority? And, by what rationale? Who are the producers of weapons of mass destruction? If there is a war, what kind of weapons will be used? Will the weapons be weapons of mass destruction? Isn't this a contradiction? There are direct links and relationships to all of these questions and the title of this book—where are the peacemakers?

There are at least 30 nations with conventional weapons—biological and chemical (selectively referred to as 'weapons of mass destruction'). The United Nations and or members of the G8 (commonly referred to as the major industrial nations of the world) should put forth the evidence in a public display and make the case. While the United Nations and or the G8 (or any of its members) puts forth evidence about who has 'weapons of mass destruction,' two additional things should be done in the process:

1. 'Weapons of mass destruction' should be clearly identified and explained (specifically, what are weapons of mass destruction?); and

2. A comprehensive list should be developed—and publicly displayed—by the United Nations—of what countries produce these weapons, state why they are produced, and to what countries the weapons are sold and or given—and why.

The primary purpose for items 1 and 2 above is to inform the world of the truth and facts—something which is missing for the 'lightweight' global discussions taking place at the moment. If these steps are taken, certain explanations and definitions provided, information about what countries are producing what, I have confidence in people's intelligence that more qualified views and comments will emerge from the current dialogue (individuals who know the facts and what they are talking about). As in any debate, dialogue, or meaningful discussion, facts are very important. Far too many people are quick to give opinions (informed, ill-informed, and uninformed). Yet, many of these same individuals are slow to ask questions. Qualified and robust debate is needed. Whether one watches CNN, BBC News, SABC Africa, read *the Guardian, Daily Mirror, the Sowetan, Washington Post, The Los Angeles Times, The Wall Street Journal, New York Times, The New York Amsterdam News, The Final Call, The Economist, The International Herald Tribune, The East African,* or *Caribbean Weekly,* try and get a look at the weapons that are being displayed in the various conflicts around the world. Weapons are not limited to one country, two countries, or even three countries. Weapons are in many countries.

As world leaders 'lead,' refuse to debate, engage in trade-offs, play politics of mass destruction, and pontificate—millions of lives are being lost and destroyed. Millions of people are left homeless, millions become refugees, and millions are internally displaced. Most of the victims are innocent children, women, men, and persons with disabilities. There are too much bloodshed and too much politics. The words of the spiritual song, What a Friend We Have in Jesus, are correct and on target, "Oh what peace we often forfeit, oh what needless pain we bear." The world is witnessing needless suffering and pain. Unfortunately, those who are causing the suffering and pain are not the ones doing the suffering. Moral leadership is needed. The politics of war is not the answer. There is a better way.

An article "Iraqi civilians will bear the brunt," in the *Baltimore Sun* (Baltimore, Maryland, USA) quoted officials from the United Nations and the World Health Organization (WHO):

> As U.S. and British forces prepare for an Iraqi war, scant attention is being paid to a looming human rights disaster: [1] if there is a war in Iraq, some 500,000 people will be killed or wounded, [2] some three million people will be displaced and separated from the families, friends, loved ones, homes, and communities, [3] out of the three million people, one million will become refugees [go to other countries] and two million people will become internally displaced within Iraq. An Arab Women's Declaration calling for a halt to military build-up cited the child mortality rate in Iraq as 130 per 1,000. An Oxford Research Group's study clearly suggests that a war against Iraq may very well lead to instability in the entire region. What about the financial costs? As if millions of lives are not enough, the American Academy of Arts and Sciences estimated that the costs of war with Iraq could amount to $1.9 trillion over a ten-year period.

War is Not the Answer

On Saturday, October 26, 2002, thousands of people took part in peaceful demonstrations and protests for peace around the world: Washington, D. C., San Francisco, California, Denver, Colorado, August, Maine (yes, a demonstration and protest in Maine)—USA, Hamburg and Berlin, Germany, Stockholm, Sweden, Copenhagen, Denmark, Rome, Italy, Tokyo, Japan, and Mexico City, Mexico, just to cite some of the cities and countries.

The demonstrations, rallies, and protests did not and will not stop there. The week of January 15, 2003 (Rev. Dr. Martin Luther King, Jr.'s birthday), mass anti-war demonstrations and rallies took place in at least twelve world capitals: London, England; Tokyo, Japan; Damascus, Syria; Cairo, Egypt; Islamabad, Pakistan; Moscow, Russia; and Washington, D.C.—USA. In fact, it was reported that demonstrators in the United States planned to march to a U.S. Navy Yard and demand the inspection of 'weapons of mass destruction.' There is more. Mass demonstrations for peace took place in 600 cities in various countries throughout the world during the weekend of February 15-16, 2003. It is estimated that more than 8 million people participated. Just as in January, people of conscience—throughout the world—continue to say no to war and yes to peace: Rome, Italy, Barcelona, Spain, one million, Madrid, Spain 650,000, London, England 500,000, in Paris, France, 100 organizations organized in 80 cities, hundreds of thousands turned out, Berlin, Germany 200,000, Damascus, Syria, Melbourne, Australia 150,000, Sydney, Australia 100,000, Cape Town, South Africa, Toronto, Canada, Dublin, Ireland, Amsterdam, Holland (the Netherlands), and Tel Avis, Israel. In the United States, protests, marches, and rallies were held in New York City, Pittsburgh and Philadelphia, Pennsylvania, Chicago, Illinois, San Diego and San Francisco, California, Detroit, Michigan and Raleigh, North Carolina (yes, Raleigh). There is much more. Demonstrations took place in South Korea, Turkey, Malaysia, Thailand, Bosnia (yes, Bosnia), Greece, Scotland, Argentina, Chile, Mexico, Peru and Puerto Rico.

Thank All Mighty God, there are people with courage and conviction who will stand up when it is time to stand up and will speak up and speak out when it is time to speak up and speak out. They are not afraid to say to their government leaders and loudly say—WAR IS NOT THE ANSWER. Six (6) members of the United States Congress, military personnel, and parents, had the conviction and courage to file a lawsuit—seeking an injunction barring an invasion of Iraq.

As is the case with many historical struggles for justice and peace—young people of the world are standing up and making their statements. In early March 2003, hundreds of thousands of school students and university students around the world took part in school walk outs, teach-ins, demonstrations, protests and rallies—all in the name of people and all against war. Activities took place in a number of countries: the United States, England, Egypt, Sweden, France, Germany, Spain, Australia, Switzerland, and Senegal (yes, two countries in Africa).

War, bloodshed, killings, and insecurity will bring about more war, more bloodshed, more killings, more destruction, and more insecurity. The ultimate security of the world is linked to love, justice, and peace—not war. Peace is brought about through justice, respect for one another, honesty, and understanding. It was encouraging to hear former South African Archbishop Tutu raise the questions: when does compassion, when does morality, when does caring come in? Archbishop Tutu raised these humane questions and concerns when commenting on the prospects of a U.S. and Britain led attack on Iraq.

In keeping with the true spirit of peacekeepers, symbolic Certificates of Peace should be awarded to the organizers, protesters and participants of the rallies and demonstrations. Those who consistently demonstrate, protest, rally, sing and organize choirs to sing, "Oh what peace we often forfeit, oh what needless pain we bare" should also be recognized as contributors to peacemaking. It is these and other individuals and similar actions that will help lead to peace—not guns, not bullets, not bombs, not fighter jets, and definitely—not political rhetoric.

In the final analysis, there is the promise of God—where it is written in the scriptures:

> If my people, who are called by my name, will humble themselves and pray and seek my face, and turn from their wicked ways, then I will hear from heaven, and will forgive their sins and heal the land (2nd Chronicles 7:14).

War is wicked. War is sinful. When nations engage in wars and when leaders of nations try to 'justify' wars—the wars are no less wicked. The wars are no less sinful. The world has witnessed far too much bloodshed and far too many wars. Give peace a chance. The ultimate security of the world is linked to love, justice, and peace—not war.

Where are the peacemakers?

CHAPTER 2

Israel and the Palestinians—July 26, 2006
The Ongoing Conflict between Israel and the
Palestinians

In early July 2006, another intense 'cycle of violence'—'cycle of vengeance'—erupted between Israel and Hamas—in the Gaza Strip of the Palestinian Territory. The cycles of violence and vengeance intensified and later spread to Lebanon—involving Israel and Hezbollah. Both Hamas and Hezbollah are Islamic organizations. Hamas is based in the Palestinian Territory. Hezbollah is based in Lebanon.

On the world stage, politicians, analysts, and news reporters define "the problem" in terms of two specific actions: 1) the capturing of an Israeli soldier by Hamas, and 2) the killing of three Israeli soldiers and capturing of three Israeli soldiers by Hezbollah. Contrary to what some political leaders, religious leaders, journalists, and academicians would try and have the world to believe—this conflict did not start in 2006. Much of the undercurrents in the ongoing conflict today between Israel and the Palestinians date back almost 100 years. Historically, aspects of the conflict date back to more than 2,000 years.

A Call to Examine the "Root Causes"

United States Secretary of State Condoleezza Rice issued a call to address the "root causes" of the ongoing conflict between Israel and the Palestinians. Secretary Rice stated that there should not be a "quick-fix solution" to the current situation. Former Israeli Prime Minister Benjamin Netanyahu, a prominent Israeli political leader, has continued to speak out about the ongoing conflict. Often, Netanyahu makes reference to the 1967 War, the 1978 Camp David Summit between U.S. President Jimmy Carter and Israeli Prime Minister Menachem Begin, the Oslo Agreement of 1993, and more. Both Rice and Netanyahu, like many other leaders, talk about the ongoing conflicts and violence by focusing only on recent history—history primarily of the past 40 years (not even 59 years). In an historical comprehensive analysis—more is required. I agree with Secretary Rice's call to address the "root causes." I disagree with Benjamin Netanyahu's narrow focus (1967 War, 1978 Camp David Summit and particularly the Oslo Agreement). What and who I agree and disagree with during this current discourse will not bring about peace. Bold and visionary peacemakers and leadership will start a genuine process leading to peace, stability, and security. The bold and visionary leadership must come from bold and courageous men, women, youth, and young adults—men, women, youth and young adults who are courageous enough to recognize and admit the truth and at the same time—not compromise the truth.

In an *International Herald Tribune* editorial, "Diplomacy's turn" (Wednesday, July 12, 2006/p. 6), it was written that:

> International diplomacy has finally started to stir in response to the havoc on both sides of the Israeli-Lebanese border, including calls by UN Secretary General Kofi Annan and Prime Minister Tony Blair of Britain for dispatching an international peacekeeping force. Stopping the fighting won't be easy, but the damages of escalating are too great to permit the major powers, or worried Arab rulers, to turn away.

In the mainstream discussions, many issues have been raised. At the same time, many important issues are not even mentioned—especially when reference is made to "root causes." If the dialogue is not broadened far beyond the current political leaders, 'key decision makers'—and timeframe of the "root causes"—key aspects and actions will not be on the agenda, i.e., the Balfour Declaration (1917) and the establishment of the current state of Israel. The Balfour Declaration laid the official international groundwork for actions which were later taken to establish the current state of Israel. Unless there are serious changes in the discourse, the political leaders and key decision makers are more inclined to look for a 'quick-fix'—again. It will simply be a case of rehashing old rhetoric. They will call it another "road map" or something and then send in an international "peacekeeping" force to keep a non-existing peace.

In order for the ongoing conflict to be addressed in a genuine and substantive way—the historical facts must be placed on the table, floor or ground for discussion. No one, two, three or four countries should determine who shall and shall not participate and what will and will not be on the agenda. In order for the conflict to be addressed in a genuine way, peacemakers are needed: peacekeepers will not suffice.

Where is the genuine leadership?

Where are the peacemakers?

Chapter 3

Israel Invades Lebanon—August 2, 2006

As innocent children, women, and men continue to die needlessly in Lebanon and other areas of the Middle East—politicians and world leaders continue to pontificate. After hundreds died, thousands were wounded, and hundreds of thousands were forced to flee from bombs and rocket attacks—"leaders" met in Rome and talked. After meeting, there was a statement released expressing "shock" at the violence, bloodshed, and killing. As people were being victimized (forced to become refugees, murdered, wounded, and internally displaced)—'world leaders' met at the United Nations (UN) and talked—again. One is left to wonder, what are the meetings about? What are they talking about? It is embarrassing and deplorable that this is the best they can do—meet and talk, meet and talk. Before concluding, they decide the next meeting—what, when, and where.

While the courageous UN Secretary General Kofi Annan tries to address the seriousness of the violence, bloodshed, killing, and suffering—politicians and 'world leaders' continue to talk. As lives continue to be lost and destroyed—the leaders continue to show the world that they value some people's lives as less important than others. Calling for meetings and discussions and more meetings and discussions is useless without addressing and solving the problems.

Where are the peacemakers? Where are the genuine leaders?

Love and *justice* are words and actions that obviously elude the vocabulary and the consciece of many of the leaders of the world. When will there be genuine efforts to address the violence, bloodshed, and killing in the Middle East? When will—as U.S. Secretary of State Condoleezza Rice put it—the "root causes" become part of the discussions and dialogue? The "root causes" of the current wave of violence will not be addressed as long as leaders and so-called leaders of the world pretend that the *Balfour Declaration* of 1917 is not an issue. When will leaders and so-called leaders of the world stop looking for "quick-fix solutions"?

In the first week after the violence erupted (July 2006), Secretary Rice spoke publicly about addressing the "root causes" of the ongoing violent and bloody conflict. After the death of many innocent children and women—hardly a word had been mentioned publicly about addressing the "root causes." As the cycles of violence continue—politicians and leaders continue to pontificate and vacillate. There is a need to trash all of the "quick-fix solutions" and get real. The destruction, violence, bloodshed, and killings are real. Real people are being murdered, wounded, and displaced. Recognizing the fact that there is a 'politics of military invasions,' where are love and justice? Where is the respect for the sovereignty of nations? As long as *love* and *justice* do not guide the framework of the dialogue—and especially the minds and hearts of the leaders of the world—the chances of peace, stability, and security being brought about in the Middle East will simply be just talk, talk, and more talk.

As the 'politics of military invasions' continues, I am reminded of what a friend and professor had to say while commenting on Where Are The Peacemakers (Chapter 2: July 26, 2006). He raised the relevant issues: "the peace," "real peace," and "generic peace." What are the differences? "The peace" which governments and those with power talk about and "real peace" or "generic peace" which ordinary people struggle for in their daily activities are not the same peace.

Those who are busy trying to keep "the peace" while ignoring "real peace" are indeed part of the problem—not part of the solution. "The peace" must first be made before it can be kept (this is common sense). The professor's position is similar to my long held belief that when some government leaders speak of peace—they are really referring to piece (with an i—not an e, a piece of this land, a piece of this or that territory, oil, diamonds, gold, uranium, strategic land for military operations, etc.). Military invasions are conducted by nations—driven by their personal, economic, and political agendas. Military invasions—with few exceptions—automatically bring about violence, destruction, bloodshed, and deaths. The logical, rationale, moral, and just thing to do is oppose ALL military invasions and occupations by one nation or nations of another nation or nations—and the violence, bloodshed, suffering, and deaths that comes with such interventions. This sounds simple—and it is. It may be difficult but it is not impossible. The approach and the process must be guided by *love* and *justice*. This clear prescription becomes clouded when politicians are placed (or place themselves) in the drivers seat.

If politicians are allowed to drive this process—without some of them stepping outside of their political skins in a forceful and compelling way—there will not be a solution, sustainable or otherwise, to the conflict in the Middle East. Many of the politicians are calling for a United Nations (UN) resolution—in New York. A UN resolution is not what is needed. A solution in the Middle East is needed—NOW. Again, a "quick-fix solution" is being sought. Again, key players who are part of the problem are trying to be part of the solution. They are trying both simultaneously. While children, women, and men continue to die needlessly—talkers continue to talk. This is shameful, senseless, and sinful. I am reminded of the words in the spiritual song, What a Friend We Have in Jesus, "Oh, what needless pain we bear." War is wicked, harmful, painful, and sinful. When nations engage in war and when 'political leaders' of nations try to justify war—war is no less wicked, no less harmful, no less painful, and no less sinful. The ultimate security of the Middle East is linked to *love* and *justice*—which lead to genuine peace. Many, if not most, of the world leaders are seriously trying to duck or side skirt the "root causes" of the ongoing conflict and violence. This approach will not bring about peace. Stop the needless suffering, bloodshed, and pain. The peace must first be made before it can be kept.

Where are the peacemakers?

CHAPTER 4

Violence and Bloodshed in the Middle East—August 10, 2006

More dead, more wounded, more internally displaced, more refugees—and they continue to talk. More rockets and bombs fall from the sky like rain—destroying, wounding, and killing—and they talk. More violence and bloodshed—and they talk. More deals and more no deals, more dead, more wounded, more internally displaced, and more refugees! Guess what? Leaders continue to talk. What about the children, women and men? What about persons with disabilities? Where are the peacemakers?

With all of the meetings, discussions, and talks by the leaders of the world, I am reminded of the profound statement by Dr. Martin Luther King, Jr. that is very appropriate regarding all the talking. Dr. King, while being held in a Birmingham, Alabama, jail in April 1963, wrote the now famous 'Letter from a Birmingham Jail.' In an attempt to try and reach certain members of the clergy and other people of "good will," he wrote the following words:

> Shallow understanding from people of good will is more frustrating than absolute misunderstanding from people of ill will. Luke warm acceptance is much more bewildering than outright rejection.

Many of the world leaders are giving a blanket endorsement to the violence, death, and destruction in the Middle East. At the same time, in their narrow minded 'lukewarm' ways, they are meeting and talking and meeting and talking—and looking for a "quick-fix solution" as they try and come up with another United Nations resolution to hide behind—again.

There was a sprinkle of hope and encouragement this past week when Pope Benedict XVI spoke out and said—"War doesn't bring any good for anybody, not even for the apparent victors." The Pope called on Christians, people of all faiths, and people in general to mobilize against warfare in the Middle East. Former United States President Jimmy Carter was much more direct in commenting on the ongoing violence by stating that President George W. Bush has pushed an "erroneous policy"—a policy which has fostered violence in the Middle East.

Out there in the 'wilderness of world leaders,' all among themselves, many are obsessed with 'the politics of war.' They believe in the idea and notion that genuine peace can and will emerge from violence, conflict, bombs, tanks, rockets, destruction, bloodshed, and death. They believe strongly in a plan which is guided by the use of force and might. As world leaders and leaders in general, more rationale thinking is expected and required. Leaders must be reminded daily that "Wisdom is better than weapons of war" (Ecclesiastes 9:18).

I submit that the current plan and course of action (paradigm) will not bring about peace, stability, or security. The current plan and course of action will help push the Middle East towards more violence, war, deaths, destruction, instability, and insecurity. Common sense should reveal this fact to 'thinking and non-thinking leaders of the world.' I further submit that those who think that 'the politics of war' will help foster peace, stability, and security have a very narrow minded view—and historical misunderstanding of the Middle East, little or no respect for most people in the Middle East, and a blind eye view of justice. The current plan and course of action will continue to bring about additional violence, bloodshed, deaths, and destruction—and no doubt—additional talk. The 'politics of war' disrespects nature and lacks moral principles.

I want to share a statement by Desmond Tutu, Nobel Laureate and Archbishop Emeritus of Cape Town, South Africa. In his book, *God Has A Dream: A Vision of Hope for Our Times* (2004), Archbishop Tutu writes,

> This is a moral universe, which means that, despite all of the evidence that seems to be to the contrary, there is no way that evil and injustice and lies can have the last word. God is a God who cares about right and wrong. God cares about justice and injustice. God is in charge.

In addition to Archbishop Tutu, Presidents Nelson Mandela and Jimmy Carter, United Nations Secretary General Kofi Annan, the Pope, and others, world leaders should be committed and compelled to loudly denounce the violence and at the same time work seriously to end the outrageous and senseless bloodshed, destruction, and killings in the Middle East. In non-political terms—there should be only one response. The response is "YES I WILL." No or I will not (inaction) speaks for itself. A political response is simply 'rhetoric'—double talk, flawed, and basically useless.

We can do better. We must do better. We must collectively—not selectively—find ways to find ways to end the violence, suffering, and killing. Courageous men, women, and youth are needed to mobilize, to step forward, and to lead. The mindset of this leadership must be guided by *wisdom, love,* and *justice.* If this is done, the peace will come.

The question of leadership is a severe issue today. In fact, the world is on the verge of suffering from a 'crisis in leadership.' Desmond Tutu's response to those who criticized his vocal and active opposition to South Africa's unjust apartheid system was—"I am compelled to say what I say." Just as the "prophets of the 8th Century BC," and as did the Apostle Paul, the message of *love* must be preached all over the world. The spirit of this peaceful approach must be adopted for the Middle East—including at the meetings where they just talk. The world leaders must be reminded time and time again—there is no 'quick-fix solution.' I am compelled to continue asking a very basic question.

Where are the peacemakers?

Chapter 5

Another United Nations Resolution is Passed—August 15, 2006

On Friday, August 11, 2006, the United Nations (UN) 15 member Security Council voted unanimously for a United States and France crafted resolution which called for an "end to hostilities in the Middle East." In other words—stop the violence, stop the killing, stop the bloodshed, and stop the massive destruction. This sounds great. It is good news to the ears. Every life-loving human being, every justice—loving human being, and every peace-loving human being in the world should be supportive of such a resolution.

The resolution, referring previous resolutions—1559 and 1680—spoke about disarmament of all Lebanese militia groups (i.e., Hezbollah), the Shebba Farms border dispute at the Lebanese—Israeli border, the release of two Israeli soldiers, more than 1,000 deaths in Lebanon and Israel since July 2006 (mostly civilians), an expanded United Nations "peacekeeping" force in southern Lebanon—perhaps as many as 15,000. The resolution calls on Israel to end all "offensive military operations" in Lebanon and for Hezbollah to stop all attacks on Israel "immediately."

As did many of the world leaders, United States Secretary of State Condoleeza Rice "welcomed the resolution." In early July, Secretary Rice called on the parties in the conflict and other world leaders to address the "root causes." She said there should not be a "quick-fix solution." In Chapter 2 (July 26, 2006), I stated, I agree with Secretary of State Rice's call to address the "root causes." I submit that 'the bridge of root causes' must be crossed at some point—sooner or later—before serious groundwork can be laid in hope of eventually reaching a 'just peace' (a new paradigm). Peacekeepers, however well intended, will not make the peace. Hopefully, this statement will not be taken as one of disrespect for United Nations Secretary General Kofi Annan, the UN, or the courageous men and women who serve on such dangerous missions. In spite of many contrary world leaders around him, Secretary General Kofi Annan has demonstrated quality leadership and courage. The painful truth is—there is no peace to keep. The peace must first be made before it can be kept. It was encouraging to hear that the two senior Archbishops in the Church of England spoke out about the ongoing violence: the Archbishop of Canterbury Rowan William and the Archbishop of York John Sentamu.

Did the United Nations Resolution Address Root Causes?

1. According to Lebanon Acting Foreign Minister Dr. Tarek Mitri, the resolution does not clarify and distinguish between "defensive" operations and actions and "offensive" operations and actions. He stated to the Security Council that a durable political solution to the crisis cannot be addressed and implemented as long as Israel continues to occupy Arab land in Lebanon, Gaza, the West Bank, the Syrian Golan Heights—and wages war on innocent people in Lebanon and Palestine.

2. The Israeli Ambassador to the United Nations stated that the resolution represented an 'opportunity to correct the mistakes of the past and create a new reality in the region.'

3. Qatar's Foreign Minister, Sheikh Hamad bin Jassen Al Thani, stated that he "welcomed the resolution." He then stated that it lacked balance and overlooked the accumulated, historical, social, and political factors that culminated in the current situation. He stated that the resolution did not address the massive destruction caused by Israel. The Foreign Minister announced that the League of Arab States will seek a "high-level Security Council meeting" for the purpose of proposing a resolution to establish a "just peace" in the region. Qatar is the only Arab country represented on the Security Council.

There are many other issues and concerns which were not addressed by the resolution:

4. There are hundreds—if not thousands—of Lebanese and Palestinians locked up in Israeli jails.

5. The resolution does not refer to the fact that Lebanese and Palestinians are being kidnapped by the Israeli Defense Force (IDF).

6. The resolution allows Israel to keep up its 'defensive operations' in Lebanon.

7. The resolution does not make reference to United Nations' resolution 242 which was passed in 1978 (28 years ago). This resolution called on Israel to withdraw from Palestinian occupied territory. The withdrawal has not happened.

8. The resolution does not reference the ongoing violence, killing, and destruction in the West Bank and Gaza by the Israeli Defense Force (IDF).

"The Bridge of Root Causes"

In the above statements, references are made to "root causes." "Does The Resolution Address Root Causes?" Eight (8) specific issues of concern are raised and highlighted. Many of the world leaders are very much aware of each of the eight issues and concerns—and more. In spite of this reality, they continue to avoid the "root causes." Sooner or later, 'the bridge of root causes' must be faced and crossed. Facing and crossing this bridge will be a very challenging, complex, and difficult task. Even though the task will be challenging, complex, and difficult, it is not an impossible one. Those who are prepared to face and cross this bridge must be genuine leaders—men, women, and youth of conviction, courage, and integrity. They must be guided by God's wisdom, love, and justice. In other words, they must be peacemakers.

What is the Prescription?

A number of 'world leaders' have stated—let us address "root causes." I sincerely agree with the calls that have been made about addressing the "root causes." Drawing on the various views in the public domain, I strongly recommend that an 'International Democratic Forum on Root Causes' be held—in the Middle East. The focus of the Forum should be addressing the 'root causes' of the ongoing cycle of violent and deadly conflict. There is no time better than the present to do so.

The criteria for such a Forum should include the following:

1. The primary focus of the Forum will be to address and examine the "root causes" of the conflict and work towards establishing a realistic and practical framework for a 'just peace.' The Forum should be inclusive—not exclusive.

2. The Forum should be broad in participation. It should include men, women, and youth leaders: politicians, scholars (religious, academicians, and legal), and representatives of various grassroots organizations. For the past 58 years, youth (boys and girls) in the Palestinian Territory (West Bank and Gaza) and Lebanon have faced armed Israeli soldiers and tanks with bricks and bottles. The youth—the future of the Middle East—have more to offer than bricks and bottles. Their critical and constructive voices must be heard.

3. No country or countries will determine who shall and shall not participate.

4. No country or countries will have veto power over any action, decision, or statements related to the Forum.

5. The participants—by consensus—will determine the agenda.

There is a better way.

Where are the peacemakers?

CHAPTER 6

Views on the Middle East Conflict—
August 18, 2006

After 34 days of violence and bloodshed in the Middle East, on Friday, August 11, 2006, the United Nations 15 member Security Council passed a resolution which called for a "cease-fire" in the violent and deadly ongoing conflict. Is the resolution a solution? Time will tell. In the meanwhile, there are mixed opinions as to what the resolution really means. There are support and reservations, and there are "what ifs" and "not without." For many—if not most—the resolution is not seen as a cure to the ongoing violent and deadly conflict (the resolution simply called for "time out"). For others—it is viewed as "something to work with"—if this is done, if that is done, if this and that discontinue. All of these views and opinions appear to be the points of different realities—different views on the Middle East—at the present time.

In a previous commentary (#5, August 15, 2006), a proposal was made which calls for the convening of an International Democratic Forum on Root Causes of the Middle East Conflict to be held in the Middle East. Unlike previous efforts—the Forum should be held 'on site,' women should be well represented and strategically situated. Unlike previous efforts, the Forum should include youth and youth leaders; unlike previous efforts, the challenge will be, as Glenn Tender calls it in *Political Thinking*, to meet a "higher standard"—one which demands "logical consistency and factual accuracy:" unlike previous efforts, no selective or self appointing nation(s) will determine the agenda, who will or will not participate, and most importantly—no nation will have veto power over positions and statements of other nations or groups.

As written previously, and worth repeating, Pope Benedict XVI spoke out recently and said, war "doesn't bring any good for anybody, not even to apparent victors." One is left to wonder, did Bob Woodward get it right in his book titled, *Bush At War*—"The No. 1 International Best Seller." It was sad to hear President George W. Bush speak on Monday, August 14, 2006, and say that 'Israel won, Hezbollah lost.' At the same time, President Bush spoke about a fragile cease-fire, he was critical of Iran and Syria—accusing both countries of backing Hezbollah. On the other hand, it is good to hear President Bush admit the bold truth and a bold challenge when he said—"we live in troubled times . . ." and then commented about leaving behind "a better world." The road towards "a better world" will not be constructed timely—if at all—if the primary focus of President Bush or any world leader or groups is centered on WHO WON and WHO LOST, especially after 1,000 deaths (mostly civilians)—many children and women, thousands of people displaced, and hundreds of thousands made refugees. In the immediate aftermath of all the suffering, pain and destruction, the timing was inappropriate for a WHO WON—WHO LOST speech. The innocent civilians in Lebanon and Israel who got caught in the crossfire—were the victims and losers. It was a lose lose situation for the innocent victims; there were no winners.

It is far past time for President Bush and other world leaders to switch off the 'war rhetoric' (this is not a call for a "time-out"). Such rhetoric will not help bring about peace. It will help make the "troubled times" even more troubling—more violent—and more insecure. The leaders must be humble and admit that "wisdom is better than weapons of war" (Ecclesiastes 9:18). Even when there are efforts made to rally around the recent UN resolution and or that UN resolution—what are the realities of the aftermaths? The leaders fail to pursue justice and peace. The leaders fail to realize and admit that war is evil and sinful. As it is written in the scriptures, "Depart from evil, and do good, seek peace, and pursue it" (Psalms 34:14). Seeking peace is good. However, it is not good enough—especially in "troubled times." Much more than is being demonstrated peace is expected and required—especially from leaders. Peace must be pursued—not just sought. There is no time better than the present to pursue it.

Many relevant issues and lessons about the "troubled times" in which we live are highlighted by former U.S. Secretary of State Henry Kissinger, in his book, *Does America Need A Foreign Policy? Toward A Diplomacy for the Twenty-First Century (2002)*. I strongly recommend that the entire Bush strategy team read, understand, and discuss this book—with an open mind. War is not the answer. The ultimate security of the world is predicated on love and justice—not war and destruction. The solution lies in justice—not bombs, rockets, tanks, and missiles. As Assistant Professor William G. Mosley wrote in *The International Herald Tribune*, "The Bush Administration is clearly better at waging war than building stable economies (see "America's lost vision, The Demise of Development," Wednesday, August 9th, 2006/page 7). The cease-fire to stop the killing and destruction is indeed welcomed and important. As recognized by knowledgeable stakeholders—it is also very fragile. Eight (8) specific issues and items were listed in the previous commentary dated August 15, 2006—under the category, 'Crossing the Bridge of Root Causes.' Two (2) more are added:

1. Since the passage of the UN resolution, France issued a call to Israel to discontinue its blockade of Lebanon's land, air, and sea. The blockade was imposed by Israel after fighting started. It is still in effect; and

2. The Lebanese Cabinet met and voted to give its 'support' to an extended personnel mission (peacekeeping mission) in southern Lebanon. It was quickly noticed by many outside of Lebanon that the cabinet's actions did not make any reference to disarming Hezbollah. The disarming of Hezbollah is a primary concern of Israel and others outside of the Middle East. Lost in all the 'diplomacy' is the fact that Israel invaded Lebanon in 1982 and formally occupied the country until 2000 (18 years of occupation). The re-entry into Lebanon did not improve relations between the two countries. The totality of circumstances must be recognized, admitted, and faced (in our analysis, we need to be "logically consistent and factually accurate"). Creating and living in a 'world of denial' does not address the realities. Wisdom and pragmatic leadership are required—if the 'bridge of root causes' is ever going to be approached and crossed.

Anatol Lieven, a senior research fellow at the New America Foundation in Washington, D.C., in a thought-provoking assessment, called on peace loving people to "Help Israel Abandon its failed strategy." He wrote:

> For whatever President George W. Bush may believe, Hezbollah is not simply a "terrorist organization" . . . it is more like the Irish Republican Army . . . which so many Americans supported for so long in their fight against the British.

The author goes on to state that,

> Hezbollah came into being in the first place to resist an Israeli invasion of Lebanon, intended to destroy the Palestine Liberation Organization. Syria supports Hezbollah in order to put pressure on Israel to give up the Syrian land it conquered in 1967 . . . So we should agree with Bush when he says that it is necessary not only to stop the immediate violence but solve its deeper roots . . . (see *International Herald Tribune*, Views/ Editorials and Commentary, Thursday, August 20, 2006/p. 7).

So, here we are again—back at 'root causes.' Sooner or later—the bridge of root causes must be faced, approached, and crossed.

Where are the peacemakers?

"Be the change you want to see in the world."

—Mahatma Ghandi

CHAPTER 7

We Live in Troubled Times—August 25, 2006

On Monday, August 14, 2006, U.S. President George W. Bush stated, "We live in troubled times." I agree with President Bush on this very important fact. In a basic and honest inquiry—people who are genuinely concerned about peace should be raising certain questions. Among the questions are these: 1) Why is the present world situation so troubling? 2) Why is there ongoing violence, bloodshed, death, and destruction in Iraq, The Middle East, Afghanistan—and other hot spots around the world? 3) Are media institutions and organizations, academic institutions and organizations, religious leaders, institutions and organizations, and civil society organizations peacefully and critically engaged? and 4) What can I do—as an individual to help improve the troubling situation, circumstances, and conditions in the world today?

In order to truthfully and sincerely tackle these questions—and more—basic and fundamental education—(and an educating process)—is needed. In the context of this discussion—education is defined and clarified. Education is the process of shaping and challenging the mind to be able to discern information and data (processing what you see, read, hear and say). Education, in this context, is broadened and is inclusive—not exclusive. Education is strongly emphasized because of its importance and the need for people to understand that many individuals are educated and at the same time they are being ill informed, misinformed, and confused.

Youth and young adults—as well as older adults who are unaware of many of the issues of the day are seeking and looking for clear and concise information that will help them better understand and articulate what the issues are. They do not need to be further ill informed, misinformed, and or confused. They need to be educated—not indoctrinated. The more informed they are—factually informed—the more they are able to contribute positively and constructively to society. There are a number of institutions and organizations that can and should help educate the people. What would help in this regard is certain words and phrases not be used as substitutes to try and explain certain issues: things, situations, circumstances, and conditions. What do I mean? Simply, I mean that using such words as "terrorist," "guerillas," "insurgents," "militants," "rebels," "extremists" and "rogue state"—without providing and establishing clear operational definitions and having those definitions placed in the public domain—becomes part a process of misinformation, name calling, and indoctrination. It is not education or educating; it is not being 'factually accurate.' Even when and if operational definitions are provided—they are used selectively (depending on who the individual is or what country it is). This is part of the problem. Individuals who are ill informed, un-informed, and misinformed are being cheated and used and are not as likely to make informed decisions and or contributions.

References are made here to several individuals who made valuable efforts to help educate all of us to make informed decisions and statements, and to ask critical questions so that we can help educate others—so that we build a "better world." Some of those individuals are Socrates, Mother Teresa, Author Ralph Waldo Emerson, Dr. Martin Luther King, Jr., (*Where Do We Go From Here: Chaos or Community?*), Rosa Parks, Historian Norman Daniel (*Heroes and Saracens*), Aung San Suu Kyi, "Prisoner of Conscience," (Nobel Peace laureate and pro-democracy leader in Burma who spent more the 13 years under "house arrest" for waging a struggle for justice and freedom), Professor Cornell West (*Democracy Matters*), Political Scientist Glenn Tinder (*Political Thinking*) and Nelson Mandela, the moral leader and peacemaker of the world—in our time.

Education means different things to different people. Education in this particular context goes back to what was written by Socrates (432-398 BC). Socrates wrote "Education." He raised a very basic question—then provided comments—"Whom, then do I call educated"? First, those who manage well the circumstances which they encounter day by day, who possess a judgment which is accurate in meeting occasions as they arise, and rarely misses the expedient course of action . . . Next, those who are decent and honorable . . . Finally, and most important of all, those who are not spoiled by their success, who do not desert their true-selves, but hold their ground steadfastly, as wise and sober-minded (men) . . .

Those who have a character . . . Socrates emphasized the importance of questions and inquiry. The leader's arena becomes much broader when certain other criteria are applied to 'conventional wisdom of leaders and experts.' It is not always the answers that ones gives that is the most important contribution—many times, it is the question one asks or fails to ask.

So, we move forward. Judgment, honor, character, sober-minded, and truth are ingredients of education. Guided by these ingredients—individuals take on different mindsets. They use judgment, they possess character, and they are sober-minded and truthful to themselves and in their dealings with others. They value their worth, they contribute, they seek information and clarification (facts and truth), they raise questions, and they think—as opposed to having others think for them. Having said this, an appeal is made for peacemakers to step forward. The fundamental requirements are thinking and commitment. Contributions can be made by the ideas you bring forth.

As Glenn Tender points out in *Political Thinking*, "Be open minded." "Ideas cannot be deliberately provided like industrial products . . . one places himself in a fundamentally wrong relationship with ideas if he conceives himself as controlling their appearance." There is room for improvement. You can contribute and make a difference. Author and literary artist Ralph Waldo Emerson issued a challenge which called for intellectual emancipation and intellectual integrity. At the same time, Emerson noted that "the hardest task in the world is to think." Professor Cornell West, *Democracy Matters*, encourages each of us to "think very carefully before accepting without question, conventional wisdom of leaders and narrow pronouncement of so-called experts." Dr. Martin Luther King, Jr. emphasized the importance of the truth. He stated, "I have tried to be honest.

To be honest is to confront the truth. However unpleasant and inconvenient truth may be, I believe we must expose the truth if we are to achieve a better quality of American life." As Dr. King was speaking to America about "American life," his message of honesty and truth is not confined to America. His message is for the world. Dr. King would go on to state that "We are now faced with the fact that tomorrow is today. We are confronted with the fierce *urgency of now* . . . . We still have a choice today: non-violent coexistence or violent annihilation. This may well be mankind's last chance to choose between chaos or community."

This statement was made 40 years ago. It reminds me of another 40 year situation where people spent 40 years wondering around in the wilderness looking for the 'Promised Land'—yet the Promised Land was just near.

Just a few years ago—at the Earth Summit in Johannesburg, South Africa—Shimon Peres, Israeli Foreign Minister was quoted as saying, "If we had Nelson Mandela in the Middle East, we would have peace." During his inaugural speech in 1994, President Mandela said to South Africa—and for men, women, boys, and girls almost everywhere to hear, "You are a child of God. Your playing small does not serve the world." Mandela's challenge to us is very simple—serve the people. Serve the world; help make a difference. The challenge reminds me of an old familiar church hymn—'A Charge To Keep' ("A charge to keep I have—a God to glorify, a never-dying soul to save and fit it for the sky—To serve the present age my calling to fulfill—Oh may it all my power engage to do thy Master's will").

Glenn Tender's challenge to each of us is crystal clear, 'higher standard,' "logical consistency and factual accuracy." Norman Daniel's contribution and challenge in this context are to help us avoid falling into the trap of what he defines as "knowledgeable ignorance." He explains that "knowledgeable ignorance" is defining a situation or thing as something it could not possibly be when the means to know the difference exists. Let us think about questions, answers, and prescriptions. Let us remember Mahatma Ghandi's challenge to us, "Be the change you want to see in the world."

1. Why is the present situation in the world today so troubling?
    Answer? There is a lack of peacemakers.
    Prescription: Think and communicate with others; create a discussion network.
    You can help make a difference.

2. Why are there ongoing violence, death, bloodshed, and destruction in Iraq, The Middle East, Afghanistan—and other hot spots around the world?
    Answer: There is a lack of peacemakers.
    Prescription: Think and communicate with others; create a discussion network.
    You can help make a difference.

3. Are the media, academic institutions and organizations, religious leaders, religious institutions and organizations, and civil society organizations playing a useful and positive role in the violent and deadly conflicts which are raging around the world?

   Answer: In some ways yes. In many ways no.

   Prescription: Think and communicate with others; create a discussion network. You can help make a difference.

As a world traveler (50 countries), spiritual, academic and pragmatic student of religion, politics, and civics—I have been exposed to a number of meetings, conferences, conventions, and classrooms where the focus was the media, colleges and universities, religious leaders, institutions and organizations, and civil society organizations. Discussions about the media often centered around these: a) What is the media? b) Who owns the media? c) What role does the media play? d) Whom is the media responsible? e) Is the media balanced? f) Is the media unbiased? and more.

Early in life, I was taught that the media has the primary responsibility of being a 'watch dog' institution for the general public. It does this by providing objective factual information which is designed to inform, to educate, and at times, to stimulate and to encourage public debate of key and critical issues and concerns (i.e., elections, crime, law, education, health, war and conflict, the economy, etc.). The activities of media houses, basically reporting the news—will end up at some point impacting on public life and public policies. In 2005, in the aftermath of September 11, 2001, journalists, editors, publishers, and other professional representatives of media institutions and organizations met in the state of California (USA) for the purpose of assessing the media's role in the Iraq War. The official position of the stakeholders at the gathering was that—'the media abdicated'—if not compromised—its purpose, duties, and responsibilities.

Having raised the three questions—offered at least one answer and a prescription for each—an equally important fourth question and challenge are raised for you to think about raising to yourself. The question for you to pose to yourself is What can I do—as an individual—to help improve the situations, circumstances, and conditions in this world—today?

Who will step forward? It is yet to be determined or demonstrated. At least one thing should be clear by now—whoever steps forward should adopt a 'strategy of love, justice, and peace': no guns, no tanks, no missiles, no jet fighters, no "smart bombs," and no other weapons of human destruction. The message and strategy should be peace—not war. Will the mission be easy? No, it will not be easy. Will the mission be difficult, challenging, and complex? The answer is yes; the mission will be difficult, challenging, and complex. In spite of the fact that the mission will be difficult, challenging, and complex—it will not be impossible.

Please be reminded that Moses had an awesome challenge, duty, and responsibility when faced with the prospects of going to Egypt on a mighty mission (a mission to tell Pharoh to let God's people go). Did Moses have reservations, apprehensions, doubt, and concerns? The answer is yes. What happened? According to the scriptures, a peacemaker named Jethro stepped forward—"And Jethro said to Moses, go in peace" (Exodus 4:18).

Where are the peacemakers? The peacemakers and potential peacemakers are out there. Who are they? Religious leaders, leaders in the academic community, leaders in civil society, leaders in the media and leaders in the public section—they are out there. Concerned women leaders and youth leaders are out there. Everyday people, the grassroots, they are out there. Some are high key and high profiled. Some are low key and low profiled. Some, potential peacemakers, are neither high nor low key, high nor low profiled. Nevertheless, they are out there. Some need prayer—sincere prayer, some need a push, and others need conviction, courage and support. In the name of justice, there is much work to be done. In the name of 'save the children,' there is need for active participants to step forward and help make genuine differences in this world, to help make this world safer and more secure. It can be done. If someone had a monopoly on getting it done, it would have been done already.

Ordinary people are making extra ordinary contributions. Ordinary people will ultimately make the major difference. Most of the 'big names' are too busy with photo ops where they make phony handshakes and seal them with phony smiles. Individuals with wisdom and courage must step forward at this critical time—or as President Bush calls it—"troubled times." At religious institutions in particular—I respectfully appeal to the congregations to clear the voices and make joyful noises and sing the harmonic messages if not the theme songs of "Ain't Gonna Study War No More" and the lines from "What a Friend We Have in Jesus," "Oh what peace we often forfeit, oh what needless pain we bear" and the words of "A Charge To Keep."

Where are the peacemakers?

CHAPTER 8

Why Do We Live in Troubled Times?— August 31, 2006

Now, more than ever—the world is in serious need of peacemakers. Why? Correctly and accurately as the condition could be described, U.S. President George W. Bush stated, "We live in troubled times" (August 14, 2006). In an announcement and statement which was picked up by major media organizations worldwide—President Bush stated, "We live in troubled times." I strongly and sincerely agree with the assessment and statement by President Bush. The primary reason for my strong and sincere agreement is because his statement is *factually accurate*.

And now, the fundamental question:

WHY?

Why do "we live in troubled times"?
Where are the peacemakers?

CHAPTER 9

Wars of Oppression and Injustice—
September 5, 2006

Conflict, turmoil, war—and threats! of more conflict, more turmoil, more wars, and more threats of wars! Children of God can do better than create conflict, turmoil, war, and destruction. What is needed? 1. A clear assessment—description if you will, 2. Peacemakers, and 3. A prescription and effective action. Can we do all three? The answer is yes—if there is the will to do so.

1. Is there relevant scripture which speaks to wars of oppression and injustice? The answer is yes:

    What causes war, and what causes fighting among you? Is it not your passion that are at war in your members? You desire and you do not have; so you kill. And you covert and cannot obtain: so you fight and wage war. You do not have, because you do not ask. You ask and you do not receive, because you ask wrongly . . . (James 4:1-3).

    Think about these profound words of scripture.

    As Pope Benedict XVI stated recently, "War doesn't bring any good for anybody, not even to apparent victors." In other words—in war—there are no winners, only losers. For the most part—those who suffer the most are innocent victims of 'the politics of war:' children, women, the elderly, and persons with disabilities. Children of God can do much better than create wars and cause unnecessary death and destruction.

I am reminded of a challenging statement by a former U.S. president:

"Every gun that is made, every warship launched, every rocket fired, signifies in the final sense a theft from those who hunger and are not fed, those who are cold and are not clothed."

President Dwight David Eisenhower
United State of America
April 16, 1953

2. *Peacemakers* are needed helpers to bring an end to death and destruction caused by 'the politics of war.' Peacemakers must make it crystal clear that the ultimate security of the world is linked to justice and peace—not war. We should be reminded of a statement by entertainer Jimi Hendrix who proclaimed that "When the power of love overcomes the love of power, the world will have peace." Is there any disagreement with this statement?

   Peacemakers should mobilize other peacemakers and say—NO TO WAR. Peacemakers should teach their children and all children to say NO TO WAR. The children should also be taught and encouraged to teach their parents, each other, their parents' friends and other adults that war is violent, bad, and dangerous—especially for children. Peacemakers must be visible and vocal in the political arena, religious institutions and organizations, in the media, in academia, in civil society, and everywhere.

3. In recognition of peacemakers and potential peacemakers—the artists: poets, dancers, film makers, play writers and other entertainers should be recognized. One of the outstanding recognition in 2006 is artist and humanitarian Bono and the rock group U2. In the international award winning album—"HOW TO DISMANTLE AN ATOMIC BOMB"—U2 gives the world part of the solution to help resist the 'politics of war'; it is effective action, a *prescription*, designed to help make peace—not war. U2, in "Love and Peace or Else,' says "lay down your guns," "we need love and peace."

Peacemakers and potential peacemakers must call for the elimination of ALL weapons of human destruction—here and now. Weapons—large and small—for the most part are manufactured for violence, death, and destruction. The manufacturing of weapons is a worldwide multi-billion dollar industry. According to the United Nations Development Programme (UNDP), Small Arms Reduction Programme, Small Arms Survey, Geneva, Switzerland (2001)—an estimated 600 companies in 95 countries are engaged in the manufacturing of small arms. According to the Omega Foundation (United Kingdom), there is an increase in countries producing small arms:

Large Arms: China, Russia, and the United States
Medium Arms: Austria, Belgium, United Kingdom, Britain, Germany, and Egypt
Small Arms: Japan, Canada, Saudi Arabia, and Sweden

Fourteen (14) countries have established small arms and ammunition licensed production with 45 other countries: Austria, Belgium, The Czech Republic, France, Germany, Israel, Italy, Portugal, South Africa, Singapore, Sweden, Switzerland, the United Kingdom, and the United States. *Information is available to the public about the weapon makers and what they are making—and for whom. Unfortunately, information is not available—and widely known about the peacemakers and their location.*

There Are Peacemaking Messages in the Music of the World

Hopefully, the manufacturing of weapons for human destruction will suggest to many that Bono and U2 make more sense than all of the politicians by simply saying—"How To Dismantle an Atomic Bomb." Bono and U2 took the message of love and peace to Bosnia and performed before a mixed audience of Muslims, Serbs, and Croats in a Sarajevo stadium—in freezing cold weather—injected the names of Dr. Martin Luther King, Jr., ("Precious Lord Take My Hand") and Ben E. King ("Stand By Me"). In addition to Bono and U2, there was John Lennon. In a one word titled song, "Imagine" (which means to picture mentally), he called attention to the mind, our mind. In the song, John Lennon said, "Imagine all the people living life in peace." He also said, "Imagine all the people sharing the world." I also want to highlight and pinpoint another peace-inspiring song. The song is titled—"From A Distance"—by Bette Midler, who "inspired the troops during the Gulf War"—in her Song of the Year (1990) says, "From a distance—God is watching us . . . from a distance, you look like my friend even though we are at war. From a distance—I can't comprehend what all this fighting is for."

As God is watching us—'from a distance'—what does God see in you and me? A few decades ago, during the Vietnam War, soulful singer Freda Payne brought a very strong message to the world. In her popular song, "Bring the Boys Home—Bring Them Back Alive"—she inspired many to voice opposition to an unpopular war. At the same time, her song was banned by many radio stations in America. There were those who felt that one can kill a message by banning the messenger. "Truth crushed to earth will rise again; no lie can live forever," said Dr. Martin Luther King, Jr.

In 2008, John Legend lent his voice and talents to call for more concern, involvement, and participation by you and me. Legend, in 'If You're Out There,' issues both appeals and challenges—a call to personal action—to let's save the world. Legend says, "No more broken promises, no more call to war, unless it's love and peace that we're really fighting for. We can destroy hunger, conquer hate, put down the arms, and raise our voices. We're joining hands today."

Where are the peacemakers?

What about the Children?

The next three commentaries will focus on the children and their plight as they are caught in poverty, wars, and war zones around the world. The children—precious, innocent and vulnerable—are the primary victims of manmade poverty, wars, violence, weapons, and destruction.

CHAPTER 10

"We Are the World"—September 29, 2006

In late 1984 and early 1985, Harry Belafonte, Ken Kragen, Quincy Jones, Stevie Wonder, Michael Jackson, and Lionel Ritchie combined their minds and talents to pull together a one of a kind gathering of artists and musicians to write, produce, and create an inspiring peace song—"We Are the World."* Talented artists and entertainers came together to touch and inspire the world: Dionne Warwick, Bob Geldolf, The Pointer Sisters, Ray Charles, Tina Turner, Kenny Rogers, Al Jarreau, Cyndi Lauper, Smokey Robinson, Bruce Springsteen, Diana Ross, Jeffrey Osborne, Bette Midler, and others. They were all carefully selected for a new and different kind of challenge. They stepped up to the plate and met the challenge. "We Are the World" became the 1985 Song and Record of the the Year—winning Grammy awards in both categories.

"We Are the World," is a peace song, focused on adverse situations, circumstances, and conditions—particularly in Africa. In the very outset of the song—the words and lyrics are pronounced.

> There comes a time when we need a certain call
> When the world must come together as one
> There are people dying . . .
> We can't go on pretending day by day
> That someone somehow will soon make a change
> We're all a part of God's great big family
> And the truth—you know—love is all we need.

---

* "We Are the World" was written by Lionel Richie and Michael Jackson. It was produced by Quincy Jones. Musicians were John Robinson, Michael Boddicker, Paulinho da Costa, Louis Johnson, Micahel Omartian, and Greg Phillinganes.

About ten years after "We Are the World" had being popularized throughout the world, Harold Melvin and the Blue Notes ('the Sound of Philadelphia') were lighting up the radio airways and concert scenes with "Wake Up Everybody" and reminding listeners that "the world won't get no better if we just let it be." Likewise, Edwin Starr was lighting it up with "War" (*"what is it good for?—absolutely nothing"*). In this world—a world in which Joe Legon and the Mighty Clouds of Joy describes as one which 'is in such sad condition—a world in such confusion' (*Steal Away*, Mighty Clouds of Joy, Live in Charleston, South Carolina, 1996). Rev. James Cleveland and the Charles Ford Singers on the album titled *Blind Man*, recorded live, "Jesus is the Best Thing That Ever Happened To Me" (Cincinnati, Ohio, 1989). Rev. James Cleveland sings so beautifully and truthfully—"We are living in such a confused world, and most folks you see can't seem to find their places . . . we are a lost generation of confused men; we're just like blind men trying to lead the blind." I must add that the point of focus there is blind, spiritually, morally, economically, and socially blind. The focus is not physically blind. There are men and women who are physically blind—yet they are not politically, spiritually, morally, economically, or socially blind. Many physically blind persons are peacemakers: Stevie Wonder, Ray Charles ("Georgia on My Mind"), Hon. Margaret Baba Diri (Member of Parliament, Parliament of Uganda), and Deacon Jessie Starks, Mt. Carmel Missionary Baptist Church, Brundidge, Alabama.

What About The Children?

In 1994-1995, The African Methodist Episcopal Church Yearbook's general theme was "Making the World Safe for Children" (Women's Missionary Society and Young People's Division). On the book's cover, in addition to the theme, the following was written: African Churches Speak (geographical theme), 1994-1995 and "Blessed are the peacemakers for they shall be called children of God" (Matthew 5:9). Written in the book's *Introduction* is the following:

> It is a human and moral travesty that more than 14.6 million children are poor, and 8 million lack health insurance in a nation blessed by such abundance and riches. Every person of

faith has a special obligation to help the poor and powerless, and to seek justice. The deepest and most enduring truth is that we must take better care of all children because it is the right and moral thing to do.

—Marian Wright Edelman
Founder and President
Children's Defense Fund
Washington, D. C.

Also in the *Introduction* is reference to the Women's Missionary Society and a listing of facts:

- 100,000 children are homeless each night.

- 145 babies are born at very low birth weight each day.

- 2,350 children drop out of school each day.

- 1,234 children run away from home each day.

- 27 children die from poverty each day.

The brief reference and statistics speak to realities in American in the 1980s and 1990s. A 2005 Children's Defense Fund Report, Protect Children, Not Guns, reveals even more staggering statistics. The report reveals that "2,827 child and teen deaths by firearms in one year (2003) exceeds the U.S. combat fatalities during the three years in Iraq." There is more:

- 56 preschoolers were killed by firearms, compared to 52 law enforcement officers killed in the line of duty.

- More 10 to 19 year-olds die from gunshot wounds than from any other cause except motor vehicle accidents.

- Almost 90 percent of the children and teens killed by firearms were boys.

- Boys ages 15 to 19 are nearly nine times as likely as girls of the same age to be killed by a firearm.

- The seven states that recorded the most deaths among children and teens by firearms were California, Texas, Illinois, New York, Pennsylvania, Florida, and North Carolina.

- The rate of firearm deaths among children under 15 is far higher in the United States than in 25 other industrialized countries—combined.

Children rights advocate Marian Wright Edelman described these alarming statistics as an "undeclared war on Children." Professor David Hemenway of Harvard University (Boston, Massachusetts—USA) stated, "We have many more handguns and much weaker gun laws than any other country."

In an article featured in the *Washington Post* titled, "The Neighborhood War Zone" by David Kennedy, Director of the Centre for Crime Prevention and Control, John Jay College of Criminal Justice, City University of New York, Kennedy highlighted devastating statistics about violence and death in American cities: Philadelphia, New York, Orlando (Florida); "Orlando's homicide count for this year reached 37, surpassing the city's previous annual high of 36 in 1982." In Washington, D.C., "14 people were killed in the first 12 days in July; Police Chief Charles H. Ramsey declared a state of emergency." In Kennedy's article, he wrote, "The United States is losing the war in Iraq. More specifically, Philadelphia is. The war is at home, in the city's 12th Police District, where shootings have almost doubled over the past year and residents have spray-painted "IRAQ" in huge letters on abandoned buildings to mark the devastation." (see *Washington Post*: http://www.washingtonpost.com/wp-dyn/content/article/2006/08/11/AR2 and or contact David Kennedy at: dakennedy@jjay.cuny.edu).

What Is Being Done?

Recently, a 'mayoral summit' was called and held to address the issues of increasing gun violence in America (April 2006). The summit was spearheaded and co-sponsored by Mayor Michael Bloomberg (New

York City) and Mayor Thomas Menini (Boston, Massachusetts). Coming out of the summit, fifteen (15) mayors from across America called for national leadership in "the war on gun violence." Since the summit, a coalition of mayors has called for action to address the problem of increasing gun violence and deaths.

What About African Children?

Innocent Victims of Conflicts, Diseases, Poverty, Wars, and War Zones?

Since the release of "We Are the World" (January 28, 1985) and the release of the African Methodists Episcopal Church's 1994-1995 Yearbook, Africa has witnessed numerous wars and violent conflicts. Millions of adults have been killed, and hundreds of thousands of children have been killed, wounded, become internally displaced, sold into servitude, become victims of child trafficking, refugees, sexually abused, and more in Sudan, Rwanda, Liberia, Uganda, Ethiopia, Eritrea, Nigeria, Sierra Leone, Kenya, Cote D'Ivoire, Angola, Somalia, Democratic Republic of the Congo (DRC), Zimbabwe, Burundi, and Namibia. Many children become victims of a 'system of child trafficking' and other forms of exploitation.

What Are The Driving Forces Behind the Conflicts and Wars?

To a large extent—if not for the most part—the systems of exploitation, conflicts, and wars are driven by *greed, corruption,* and *mismanagement* by African leaders—supported by their 'partners in crime' from outside the African Continent. The theft and mismanagement of resources—human and natural—are robbing the children of valuable resources needed for education, health, recreation, and life.

According to the Stockholm (Sweden) International Research Institute, global military spending has reached $1.12 trillion—with the United States accounting for 48% of the spending. Spending for weapons accounts for 2.5% of the world's gross domestic products, average spending is $173 per capita. Following the United States in weapons spending is the United Kingdom (UK), France, Japan, and China.

What IF these resources were spent on children and their welfare? education? health? recreation and life?—as opposed to death. The children of Africa are being victimized and marginalized by many of their leaders. The leaders do not spend $173 annually per capita (the amount spent on weapons)—on education, health and recreation combined. The leaders are spending their scarce resources on bullets, bombs, tanks, and missiles as opposed to education, health, and recreation.

In spite of this dismal and chaotic reality, you can help support the children more. Hopefully, you will do as they said in *We Are the World*—and 'lend a hand.' Each one of us can 'lend a hand.' In the process of doing many types of activities and interventions—there is need to be *factually informed*. Information is readily available on the worldwide web (www), in magazines, newspapers, on radio, and at think tanks—locally, regionally, nationally, and internationally:

The Cradle, The Children's Foundation, Promoting Justice for Children

House 2

Wood Avenue

P.O. Box 10101-00100 GPO

Nairobi, Kenya—East Africa

Tel: 250 (0) 20 3874576 Fax 250 (0) 202710156

E-mail: info@thecradle.or.ke

> www.thecradle.or.ke
> See *"Making Children Count"* (November 2004)

The Regional African Juvenile Justice Network

> www.africajuvenilejustice.net

The United Nations Children Education Fund (UNICEF)

> www.un.org

The United Nations Commission on Human Rights (UNHCR)

> www.un.org

The United Nations World Health Organization (WHO)

> www.un.org

American Friends Services Committee

> www.afsc.org

The Cost of Wars Since 2001 (Iraq and Afghanistan), The National Priorities Project, http://nationalpriorities.org

www.costofwar.com

Center for Nonproliferation Studies, Monterey Institute of International Studies www.cns.miis.edu

The Children's Defense Fund

25 E Street, NW

Washington, D.C. 20001

Tel: (202) 628-8787 Fax: (202) 662-3510

E-mail: cdfinfo@childrensdefense.org

www.campaignchildrendefense.org/links.aspx

The State of America's Children 2005

"13 million poor children in America"

"The African Center on the Rights and Welfare of the Child (ACRWC)

www.africaninstitute.org

African Women for Peace

"Gender Justice in Post-Conflict Countries in East, Central and Southern Africa"

University of Pretoria

Pretoria, South Africa 0002

Tel: +27 12 4203810 Fax: +27 12 3625125

www.chr.up.ac.za

Women Building Peace

www.womenbuildingpeace.org

United Nations Development Fund for Women
Women's International League for Peace and Freedom

www.wilpf.org

Women Waging Peace

www.womenwagingpeace.com

"The UN Study on Violence Against Children"

www.unhchr.ch/html/menu2/6/crc/study.html

One Voice
www.onevoicemovement.org

www.onevoice.com

www.onemillionvoices.com

One Voice Movement for Peace

Whether one listens to artist and entertainers singing "We Are the World," Harold Melvin and the Blue Notes singing, "Wake Up Everybody"—"The world won't get no better if we just let it be," Joe Legon and the Mighty Clouds of Joy singing about "the sad conditions of this confusing world," or children rights activist and defender of children's rights, Marian Wright Edelman saying "the deepest and most enduring truth is that we must take better care of all children because it is the right thing to do," leaders of the world who are architects and supporters of 'the politics of war' must show and demonstrate concerns for all children—not just their own children who are 'physically secure and protected' from the wars, death, weapons, and destruction created by adults.

Where are the peacemakers?

Chapter 11

"Children Are a Gift from God"—
November 5, 2006

This commentary is the second of a three part series focusing on children and their plight as they are caught up in poverty, wars, and war zones around the world. The children—precious, innocent, and vulnerable—are the primary victims of manmade poverty, wars, violence, and destruction.

Children are a gift from God

—Psalm 127:3

From my travels, exposure and experience, much has been *seen, heard,* and *read.* Information was provided in the previous commentary (September 29, 2006): statistics, organizations, websites, telephone numbers, fax numbers, e-mail addresses, physical addresses, and more. The commentary encouraged and appealed to individuals of good will, institutions, organizations, hearts, and minds—to become more informed, knowledgeable and contribute, make a genuine difference in this world—especially children's world. More of the same is offered in this written commentary; it presents poetry and art by children who have experienced war and war zones. Often times—we as adults listen and learn—then we tell the story, the children's story. We need to recognize children's ability to tell their own story. They can inform and educate us—all of us. We can learn from the children—God's gift. (See poetry, drawings and illustrations by children from Gulu, Uganda, the Republika Serpska—*Wounded Childhood*, and the United States of America.)

A violent, bloody and deadly war took place in Bosnia & Herzegovina. The war was described as a war of "ethnic cleansing"—three ethnic groups killing and destroying one another. Millions of people were killed and injured, hundreds of thousands became internally displaced and/or refugees (refugees from Bosnia & Herzegovina were located in at least 80 countries during the following the war).

РАНЕНО
АЛЕТННСТВО

A book called РАНЕНО АЈЕТННСТВО (translation meaning "WOUNDED CHILDHOOD") contains this picture of a little boy in tears, the sun shining (in tears) above and behind the boy, and a poem with a dove. The displays: pictures, symbols and poem, are expressions, feelings and concerns depicted by children (pictures, expressions, feelings and concerns that are brought about as a result of war and destruction). This book was given to Jerry Henderson in Zvornik, Republic of Serpska. The following complimentary message was written in the book, "to honest and dear friend, with respect."

Јако Ерлелић, VIII-

Рат

Рат је прљава мржња
који оставља
крвави трат,
у срцу мене,
у срцу тебе,
у срцу свих нас.

Вуковић
Марина II-2

Рањено дјетињство

Приредио:

Радосав Перић

Iskrenom i dragom
prijatelju
Jerry Henderson

S poštovanjem.

Zvornik, 1. vi 1997. *Radosav Perić*

CREATIVE: An IDP camp on fire asdepicted in a painting by Gulu children

CREATIVE: An IDP camp on fire as depicted in a painting by Gulu children

Children illustrate grave situation in IDP camps

By Roderick Ahimbazwe

As peace talks between the LRA rebels and the Government intensify, children are busy agitating for return of peace in the region. The children have been unable to go to school and others had to starve. The children held an art exhibition at Makerere Art Gallery recently highlighting the situation in IDP campus. Olee William, 13, told of how they suffered in LRA captivity. The children appealed to the Government to reach an agreement with the rebels so to return peace to the region. The paintings showed how rebels used to attack the villages.

Steven Smyhtes of One Dream, an NGO that cares for the children said the children are bright and need education just like other children in the country.

The New Vision
Kampala, Uganda
Friday, September 22, 2006/p. 21

"Children illustrate grave situation in Internally Displaced People's (IDP) Camps" *The New Vision* newspaper featured an article, "ART Ahimbisibwe's work speaks without words." In the article are words and pictures—drawings by children. It was written:

> As peace talks between the LRA rebels at the Covenant intensify, children are busy agitating for return to peace in the region. The children have been unable to go to school and others had to starve. The children held an art exhibition at Makerere Art Gallery recently highlighting the salvation in IDP Camps. (IDP is the acronym for internally displaced people). See: *The New Vision*, "Children illustrate grave situation in IDP camps" Kampala, Uganda, Friday, September 22, 2006, p. 21. (http://www.newvision.co.ug).

Earlier this year, Oprah Winfrey (Oprah Winfrey Show) devoted her highly acclaimed and much watched television show to help expose, educate and inform people of the world about the 22 year long conflict in northern Uganda. Oprah aired a documentary, the Invisible Children. The documentary highlighted what are commonly referred to as "night commuters." There is a sad history about "night commuters."

According to the *New Vision*, "Every night, the children flee their unsecured rural houses in Gulu districts to sleep on shop verandahs in the town" (See: *The New Vision*, "Oprah, pleads for Acholi," Kampala, Uganda, Tuesday, May 2, 2006, p. 1 and the *Daily Monitor*, "Hundreds in U.S. Sleep in the Cold for Gulu Children," Kampala, Uganda, Saturday, April 29, 2006, p. 1, (http://www.monitor.co.ug).

Where are the peacemakers?

As young and victimized as they are—children—through their statements, poetry, and drawings are clearly peacemakers and they should be viewed as a significant part of the peacemaking process.

Where are the peacemakers?

Oprah Winfrey is a peacemaker and contributor of time, talent, money, and more. Oprah has contributed—consistently—to many worthwhile causes. It was stated in *The New Vision* newspaper that "over 300 million television viewers around the world witnessed the tragedy of The Northern Uganda War victims, as it was featured last week on the world's biggest talk-show, the Oprah Winfrey Show." The article stated that, the host, Oprah, a human rights activist and philanthropist, described the situation in northern Uganda as a holocaust saying since she saw the horrible pictures, she had been suffering sleepless nights. Oprah called upon viewers to rise up against the madness and help curb the atrocities happening in Africa. (Reference is made to Sudan as well, Darfur in particular).

Children are the primary victims of war.

Their voices should be heard.

Their drawings and illustration—their expressions—should be displayed and addressed.

Where are the peacemakers?

Women's Missionary Society and Young Peoples Division

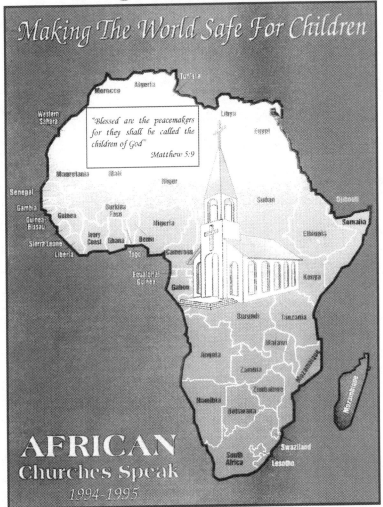

Making The World Safe For Children

"Blessed are the peacemakers for they shall be called the children of God"
Matthew 5:9

AFRICAN
Churches Speak
1994-1995

African Methodist Episcopal Church 1994-1995
YEARBOOK

Making the World Safe for Children

In the *African Methodist Episcopal Church 1994-1995 Yearbook*, Women's Missionary Society and Young People's Division, the general Theme was "Making the World Safe for Children." The Yearbook was filled with comments, suggestions, recommendations, poetry, and biblical scripture. There was a poem titled, *The Beautiful Children*, it was written by Fanta Gibson, 13 years of age, Thirteenth Episcopal District.

The beautiful children

Who have done nothing wrong

Should not have to live in chaos
for so long

If the world is dying,
could mankind be the cause?

We must come together
or it will be everyone's loss

Save the children!
if not now, then when?

We should not love everything
before we even begin.

We were put on this earth for a purpose
by the gracious Father above.

We shall stop the hole that's spreading
and start wind each day in love.

Save the World for the children!

It is the least that should be done.

If we pray and work in harmony,
the battle can be won.

If we write and put God first,

We can reduce the hold of sinners.

Victorious over all!

We are the ones who will be winners!

—Especially the children . . .

The beautiful children.

CHAPTER 12

The Children of Sudan—December 15, 2006

This commentary is the third in a three-part segment which focuses on children in poverty, wars, and war zones around the world. The children—precious, innocent, and vulnerable—are the primary victims of manmade poverty, wars, violence, weapons, and destruction.

Where are the peacemakers?

War, violence, death, destruction, and bloodshed are daily realities in many countries. Adults continue to offer justifications for murder. Children continuously are the primary victims. Sudan, Africa—Darfur in particular—is a case in point. In Sudan, thousands of children have been kidnapped, raped, sold into slavery, injured, and or killed. Recently, children were rounded up, forced into a structure (a hut), and burned to death [similarly to a sad incident that took place in Rwanda, Africa, during 100 days of genocide, 1993].

After many years of little or no media coverage and exposure by the major media networks, NBC television aired a special series which focused on Darfur ("Crisis in Darfur"). A portion of the series featured interviews of children conducted by personnel from the United Nations (UN), the United Nations Children Education Fund [UNICEF]. As demonstrated and illustrated in *"Where Are The Peacemakers?"* #11 (November 5, 2006), children have a way of stating their plight and concerns with clarity (United States of America, Uganda, and the Republic of Serpska).

In an examination of children's art work and expressions in Darfur—the interviewers revealed that when children were in school *prior to the war*, they drew and painted bright colorful pictures (pictures of joy and positive activities). Since the ongoing war in Darfur, many of the children—sometimes the same children—are now drawing and painting pictures of negativity and sadness: *bombs, guns,* and *dead bodies.* Wars have physical and psychological effects on the children.

There are a number of individuals, institutions, and organizations working on behalf of children. There is plenty of work to do. There is plenty of room for YOU. You can get more specific information and then decide what you can and will do concerning this humanitarian crisis. You can contact any of the following organizations:

- "Crisis in Darfur" http://www.nightly.mnbc.com

- The United Nations Children Education Fund (UNICEF)

  http://www.un.org

- The African Centre on the Rights and Welfare of the Child (ACRW)

  http://www.africaninstitute.org

- The Regional African Juvenile Justice Network

  http://www.africajuvenilejustice.net

- The Cradle, The Children's Foundation

- Promoting Justice for Children

  http://www.thecradle.com

Politically speaking, something must be *said* and *done* in order to help make sure that the humanitarian support is balanced with realistic strategies. In Addis Ababa, Ethiopia this past month, UN Secretary General Kofi Annan—working alongside representatives from the African Union (AU), the European Union (EU), China, Russia, France, the Arab League, Sudan, and other countries—met and discussed the violent and deadly crisis in Darfur. While Kofi Annan has displayed bold courage and leadership around the world, there are clear identified problems and challenges regarding proposed strategies for ending the crisis in Darfur:

- The political will does not exist among the leaders and nations that met and continue to meet and meet and meet to address what Secretary General Kofi Annan calls a 'fragile and volatile situation.'

- Secretary General Kofi Annan's proposal which calls for a 20,000 member UN peacekeeping force does not provide a realistic, practical, and workable plan or framework to address the fact that there is 'no peace to keep.'

- There is reluctance on the part of most world political leaders to take immediate and direct actions against Sudan government in Khartoum and the violent henchmen known as the Janjaweed—which is supported by the Sudan government.

For the sake of the children especially, where are the peacemakers?

CHAPTER 13

A Tribute to Kofi Annan, Secretary General of the United Nations: 1996-2006—December 31, 2006

After serving as Secretary General of the United Nations (UN)—"world's top diplomat" for the past ten (10) years, Kofi Annan's service to the 192 member nation's organization comes to an end in January 2007. In his efforts to lead the world organization that is ". . . central to global efforts to solve problems that challenge humanity"—Kofi Annan—like many leaders, had his high points and his low points. Speaking at the Truman Library in Independence, Missouri (December 11, 2006) and the UN General Assembly (September 19, 2006), Secretary General Kofi Annan reflected on his past 10 years at the UN. He talked about the UN's humanitarian and developmental actions: the 'oil-for-food' scandal that plagued the UN, reforms at the UN, and he cited the failure to stop the Iraq War as the worst moment of his 10 years in office. At the Truman Library he called for a 'new and urgent push for peace' in the Middle East. At the United Nations General Assembly, he stated, "I remain convinced that the only answer to this divided world must be a truly United Nations." Consistently, from Africa to the Middle East and other parts of the world, these two statements are testimonies to the courageous leadership displayed by Kofi Annan during his entire tenure as Secretary General of the United Nations.

Kofi Annan is indeed a peacemaker.

Chapter 14

Rev. Dr. Martin Luther King, Jr.— January 15, 2007

By design, commentary # 14 is written and dated January 15, 2007. It is written in January—the first month of the year for specific reasons. It is dated January 15, the 78th birthday of the late Dr. Martin Luther King, Jr. who was often referred to in life—and in death—as "a drum major for justice." Dr. King, a 'drum major for justice,' was a peacemaker. He preached and practiced love, respect for one another—and justice. He encouraged others to do the same.

January is the start of yet another year. It affords many of us opportunities to look back and reflect—reflect on the previous year and years, to think, to contemplate, to question, and to attempt and chart innovative, varied, and better courses for 2007 and beyond. January is a time when we can and should recall the end of the previous year: what went well, what went not so well, what went bad, and what went very badly. Reflecting on 2006 and these items—the issues and subject of weapons (military and otherwise) and their use and impact comes to mind. What went well in 2006 cannot realistically be attributed to weapons. Much of what went bad in 2006 can be attributed to weapons. What went not so well in 2006 can in part be attributed to weapons What went very badly in 2006 can and should be attributed to weapons.

Earlier commentaries focused on the manufacturing, use, and distribution of weapons—especially in relationship to human destruction (loss of life, individuals being wounded, internally displaced, being made refugees, and property being destroyed). What is the solution regarding weapons? If world leaders and stakeholders are genuinely concerned about the welfare of all human beings, all weapons must be destroyed. All God-loving and God-fearing people should accept this premise. Why? It is the right, moral, and just thing to do. Reflecting back beyond 2006, on Saturday, December 30, 2006, a television network aired segments of a Rev. Billy Graham sermon ("Billy Graham Classic"). The network captured Rev. Billy Graham delivering a sermon in Chicago, Illinois, in 1962 (a year before Dr. King led the historic March on Washington, D.C.). In his sermon, Rev. Graham told the audience, "military might will not save us. Only God can save us (http://www.billygraham.org/tv).

As a nation, America is 45 years older since Rev. Billy Graham spoke in Chicago, Illinois, and Dr. Martin Luther King, Jr. led the historic March on Washington, D. C. America had a golden opportunity to alter some of its flawed policies—especially foreign policies—that have been coming from Democratic and Republican administrations in Washington, D.C. If this is done, America and the world can be on the road to genuine peace and security.

CHAPTER 15

President George W. Bush Calls for More Troops in Iraq—January 22, 2007

On Wednesday, January 10, 2007, President George W. Bush addressed the American people concerning Iraq and the ongoing bloody, violent, and deadly conflict. I, like many other American citizens, listened to what he had to say and have questions and opinions. According to President Bush, more troops are needed in Iraq to help fight "the global war on terror."

Since the September 11, 2001, violent and deadly attacks against America, President Bush concentrated his attention primarily on Iraq, President Saddam Hussein, and "weapons of mass destruction." At the same time President Bush was focusing his primary attention on Iraq, President Saddam Hussein, and "weapons of mass destruction," and many other voices (including voices within his administration) were calling for primary focus on Osama Bin Laden and Al-Qaeda. President Bush contended that there was a direct connection between Iraq, "weapons of mass destruction," Al-Qaeda—and the violent and deadly attacks of September 11 in New York, Pennsylvania, and Washington, D. C. After a number of inquiries, studies, interviews, and reports—no factual links were established between Iraq, President Saddam Hussein, "weapons of mass destruction," Al-Qaeda—and the violent and deadly attacks of September 11th. It is important that these series of events and circumstances be pointed out because herein lies the basis for policies, decisions, and actions that have tied the United States and Iraq together since March 2003. President Bush's speech on Wednesday, January 10, 2007, mentioned and alluded to some of these points. Drawing on this background, there is a very important lesson to be learned and shared. The lesson, using an illustration, is this: The invasion of Iraq in March

2003 was a major mistake in judgment. It was tantamount to building a house or structure on quicksand. Logic and common sense dictate that any structure which is built on quicksand will start to sink immediately. The sinking may not be noticeable to the naked eye. However, using the proper instruments, the sinking can be measured. Whether one uses logic, common sense, or the proper instruments for measuring, objects placed on quicksand will sink. The "surge" by President Bush, placing 21,500 more U.S. military personnel (and equipment) in the quicksand (Iraq) will not stop the sinking. Less is needed—not more. The sinking will continue—2007, 2008, 2009, and beyond. The rational approach to use when trapped in quicksand is this:

1. Recognize the fact that you are in quicksand, and

2. Develop an immediate strategy (exit strategy) for getting out.

There is need for a carefully designed and implemented exit strategy—NOW.

Where are the peacemakers?

CHAPTER 16

America's Security—January 26, 2007

"What happens in Iraq matters to your security here."

—U.S. President George W. Bush
Washington, D.C.
January 19, 2007

Again, I strongly agree with a statement by President George W. Bush, during a *USA Today* interview; he stated "What happens in Iraq matters to your security here" ("Bush: Iraq war plan will prove its worth," *USA Today*, Monday, January 22, 2007, p. 1). Why do I agree with the statement by President Bush? My response is very simple. The statement is factually accurate.

In regards to the statement, I am reminded of a statement by Dr. Martin Luther King, Jr. when he said to the nation and the world, "Injustice anywhere is a threat to justice everywhere." Clearly—there is an international wind of injustice flowing in parts of the world today. Injustices (violence, death, poverty, and destruction) are inflicted on millions of innocent people worldwide who have little or nothing to do with 'the politics of war' being waged by their leaders. They are victims. There are clearly identified victims of injustices in Iraq, the Palestinian Territory, Israel, Lebanon, Sudan, Ethiopia, Eritrea, Haiti, Nigeria, and the United States—yes the United States. In March 2003, the United States led an invasion into Iraq. The 'justification' given for the invasion was that Iraq was manufacturing and stockpiling 'weapons of mass destruction.' Four years later—after much bloodshed, death, and destruction—no such weapons have been located or produced. During the past two years, the 'justification' given for remaining engaged in Iraq is to help liberate Iraqis (introduce Iraqis to democracy).

On the global state, the 'justification' given for the invasion of Iraq has not been backed by evidence. Emerging more and more each day on the regional stage is suspect, skepticism—if not outright rejection of the idea that the interest and commitment now is about democracy in Iraq. According to *The Iraq Study Group Report*, which was issued in 2006, "most of the region's countries are wary of U.S. efforts to promote democracy in Iraq and the Middle East" (p. 28). When the Middle East is referenced, a number of other countries, territories, and issues become part of the discourse (or at least should become part of the discourse): Iran, Syria, Saudi Arabia and the Gulf States, Afghanistan, Lebanon, Israel, and the Palestinian Territory. As stated very clearly in *The Iraq Study Group Report*, "Iraq cannot be addressed effectively in isolation from major regional issues, interest, and unresolved conflicts. To put it simply, all key issues in the Middle East—the Arab-Israeli conflict, Iraq, Iran, the need for political and economic reforms, and extremism and terrorism—are inextricably linked" (p. 44).

Dr. Martin Luther King, Jr. reminded America and the world that people, territories, and nations are interrelated—what affects one affects all. Within this context, I must strongly agree with Dr. King as well as President Bush's statements, "What happens in Iraq matters to your security (here)." Americans—informed and engaged—can influence the ultimate reality of that security. Will Americans demand a fundamentally new approach in Iraq? Some individuals argue that voters sent a call for a 'new approach' to the nation leaders in Washington, D.C., on Tuesday, November 7, 2008, during the general election.

Where are the peacemakers?

CHAPTER 17

President George W. Bush's State of the Union Address: The War in Iraq—January 31, 2007

On Tuesday, January 23, 2007, U.S. President George W. Bush delivered his 7th State of the Union Address to the United States Congress and the American people. Just as many other Americans, I listened to the entire speech. I did so because it was part of my civil education and responsibility. The speech was basically delivered in two parts. One part addressed domestic issues, and one part addressed international issues—namely "the war on terror"—the War in Iraq. While defending his "new strategy" in Iraq and calling on the United States Congress and the American people to give his proposed strategies of Wednesday, January 10, 2007, a chance (President Bush had earlier called for the deployment of 22,000 additional U.S. troops in Iraq).

I submit that the most profound statement during his speech came when he stated:

> This war is more than a clash of arms—it is a decisive struggle, and the security of our nation is in the balance. To prevail, we must remove conditions that inspire blind hatred, and drive 19 men to get onto airplanes and come and kill us . . . . We advance our own security interest by helping moderates, reformers, and brave voices of democracy. The great question of our day is whether America will help men and women in the Middle East to build free societies and share in the rights of all humanity. And I say, for the sake of our own security—we must.

I strongly agree with this very important statement by the President—with one exception. Indeed, America's security—at home and abroad—is at risk. President Bush recognizes this 21st Century reality. However, he and many other leaders of the nation have not seriously analyzed (or understood) why America is at risk. This gap, if you will, is what helps to form the basis of my one exception. The one exception to President Bush's assessment is that America's security—or insecurity—is not a result of "blind hatred." To state that the problem is "blind hatred" of America is to underestimate and over simplify the present reality in the world today.

In 2003, a book, *Why Do People Hate America?* by Ziauddin Sardar and Merryl Wyn Davies (journalists, writers, and former British Broadcasting Company—BBC investigators)—was released in the United Kingdom. The book, an international bestseller, provides an historical and descriptive thought-provoking analysis—from Wounded Knee to many other situations in countries, territories, and locations around the world. It explores the impact of America's foreign policy. In a written statement of the book's cover, distinguished scholar and Professor Noam Chomsky states the book "contains valuable information that we should know, over here, for our own good and the world's."

As stated on a website, "their analysis provides an important contribution to a debate which needs to be addressed by people of all nations, cultures, religions, and political persuasions—and especially by Americans." The President stated that he will propose to establish a special advisory council on "the war on terror" made up of leaders in Congress from both parties. I recommend that this book, as well as other similar books, reports, papers, and studies, should be given serious attention and study by President Bush, his advisors, members of Congress, staff of Congress, and the American people.

The President stated, "American foreign policy is more than a matter of war and diplomacy. Our work in the world is also based on a timeless truth: To whom much is given . . ." I agree with the President's "timeless truth." I read that statement (verse) in the *Bible*, Luke 12:48. There is another part to the verse—'to whom much is entrusted much is expected.' It is expected that "leaders" find a way to find a way to pursue peace—now.

Where are the peacemakers?

CHAPTER 18

Anti-Iraq War March and Rally in Washington, D.C.—February 3, 2007

On Saturday, January 27, 2007, tens of thousands of people marched and rallied in Washington, D.C.—at the National Mall—in order to voice their objections to the ongoing killings, bloodshed, and destruction in Iraq. People came—soldiers, families of soldiers, veterans, grandmothers, grandfathers, mothers, fathers, sisters, brothers, school children, activists, celebrities, members of the U.S. Congress, and more—from various parts of the United States to demonstrate and protest President George W. Bush's handling of the war in Iraq.

A number of individuals spoke during the three hour activity. The youngest speaker at the National Mall, Mariah Arnold, a 12 year old, said, "Now we know our leaders either lied to us or hid the truth. Because of our actions, the rest of the world sees us as a bully and a liar." Voicing similar comments, California Congresswoman Maxine Waters said the President "tricked" the country into war by not telling the truth. On the same day, thousands of people marched and rallied in the state of California. Demonstrations, protests, rallies, and other anti-Iraq war activities are scheduled to take place in at least 25 U.S. cities during February.

As resistance to President Bush's war plan is gaining momentum in the U.S. Congress and throughout the nation, the President continues to push forward with a kind of attitude that suggests that we 'give war a chance.' In response to the opposition to Bush's plan, U.S. Secretary of Defense Robert M. Gates has stated that certain actions that are being taken in Congress will "embolden the enemy." Senator Joseph Biden, Jr. Chairman of the Senate Foreign Relations Committee, gave an appropriate response when he stated, "It is not the American people or the U.S.

Congress who are emboldening the enemy. It's the failed policy of this President—going to war without a strategy, going to war prematurely."

The invasion of Iraq was a very bad decision (see *Commentary #1*, March 2003, Revised). The people of the United States voiced their opposition to The Iraq War then and on Tuesday, November 7, 2008, during the last general election. Hopefully, the leaders of the nation will move beyond rhetoric and address this issue in a substantive way. Stevie Wonder raised a relevant and timely question in one of his many hit songs, "Blowing in the Wind." He says, ". . . How many ears must one man have before he can hear people cry? How many deaths will it take till he knows too many people have died?"

Where are the peacemakers?

CHAPTER 19

The Israeli and Palestinian Conflict: Another Meeting—February 5, 2007

On Friday, February 2, 2007, the so-called diplomatic Quartet met in Washington, D.C., for the stated purpose of addressing the Israeli-Palestinian conflict and the long-discussed proposed 'Road Map to Peace.' The Quartet, represented by the United States, Russia, the European Union (EU), and the United Nations (UN), continues to meet—again and again—and talk. They talk about Israel, the Palestinians, and about 'a two state solution'—which was supposed to be a done deal in 2005. They talk about a 'Road Map to Peace.' Unfortunately, there are some very basic and fundamental facts and issues that they are not inclined to address.

The idea and concept of 'a road map' towards peace is a good one. The Quartet and others must be aware that there are basic and fundamental requirements in the art of sound road construction: 1) have a clear knowledge and understanding of the surface for which the road is to be constructed; 2) make sure that the foundation on which the road is going to be built is solid; and, 3) do not take short cuts. It remains to be seen whether the Quartet is aware of either requirement.

Knowledge, understanding, foundation, and shortcuts can be summed up in what is not being adequately discussed or addressed by the Quartet. These issues and concerns were raised in a previous commentary (# 2: "*Israel and the Palestinians*," July 26, 2006). The issues and concerns have not changed. The fact of the matter is, at some point in the process of meetings and discussions, the 'bridge of root causes' must be honestly and properly discussed, faced, addressed, and crossed. To continue to do otherwise is to look for a shortcut or quick fix. The facts are contained in the records (*the Balfour Declaration*, [1917], United Nations Resolutions

242, 338, and other Resolutions, the establishment of the state of Israel in 1948, the 1967 War, Camp David Accords, 1978—and more). Countries and territories were invaded and occupied. Arab (Palestinians) land was taken. There is occupation by the Israeli military. Israel has consistently violated international law. Arabs (Palestinians) have died, been wounded, been displaced, and are imprisoned in Israeli jails (thousands of men, women, and children are held in jail). Palestinians are internally or externally displaced (refugees). There is the need to be factually accurate and logically consistent. The Quartet is not doing either. The Quartet does not involve the key players—Israelis, Palestinians, and others in the Middle East—in the meetings and discussions regarding the conflict and its resolution.

There are major gaps in "the Road Map" concept, a concept initiated by President George W. Bush and later introduced by UN Secretary-General Kofi Annan (April 2003). The "Road Map," in part, is based on the premise that the conflict between the Palestinians and Israelis started in and around 1967. Fundamental pre and post 1967 issues and conditions are not sufficiently addressed (Palestinians' rights, land, and territory). Even with this reality, the Palestinians accepted "the Road Map" concept and proposal as presented. On the other hand, the Israeli government responded with a long list of conditions and prerequisites—not recognizing Palestinians rights, land, or territory. All of these relevant issues must be addressed at some point—in order for peace and security to become a reality.

Following the Quartet's meeting of Friday, February 2, 2007, a prepared statement was read by UN Secretary-General Ban Ki-Moon (http://www.un.com). The next meeting of the Quartet is scheduled to take place in Berlin, Germany. Yes, another meeting.

Where are the peacemakers?

CHAPTER 20

Palestinians Meet in Mecca, Saudi Arabia— February 14, 2007

Palestinian leaders of Hamas and Fatah met in Mecca, Saudi Arabia last week in efforts to address and halt internal violence, bloodshed, and death by Palestinians. The two organizations reached a tentative agreement which calls for power sharing in a Palestinian government of national unity.

High level meetings were held between Palestinian President Mahmoud Abbas (Fatah), Hamas leader Khaled Meshaal, and Palestinian Prime Minister Ismail Heniyeh. Underlining causes of the differences and conflict between Hamas and Fatah are many, including ideological and philosophical. Fatah is the party of the late Yasser Arafat and the Palestine Liberation Organization (PLO). Fatah represents the old guard. Hamas, formed later after Fatah, represents the new guard. For more than three decades, Arafat served as the free and democratically elected leader of the Palestinian people—from 1966 until his death in 2004 as the President of the Palestinian Authority. In the January 2006 Palestinian Authority elections, Hamas won a majority of the seats in parliament (77 out of a total of 132 or 58.33%. Fatah won 45 or 34.9%). Both Fatah and Hamas were born in opposition to Israeli invasions and occupation of Arab land—in particular the West Bank and Gaza Strip, i.e., *root causes* (PLO in 1964 and Hamas in 1987). From its beginning, the PLO's major objective was the establishment of a Palestinian state.

Adding to the enormous complexity of the current conflict between the two is overt western interest and influence that is magnified by 'lukewarm' support of President Abbas (Fatah) and outright rejection of Hamas. This interest and influence is reflected mostly by the United States and parts of Europe. The U.S. initiated and pushed for an embargo against Hamas, after the organization was successful in the January 2006 elections. It is worth pointing out that during President George W. Bush's administration in particular, the U.S. has opposed both Fatah (Yasser Arafat/PLO) and Hamas. At this point, whatever agreements are reached between Fatah and Hamas are subject to acceptance and or rejection by the U.S., Israel, and others. In the aftermath of the meeting in Mecca last week, a meeting is scheduled to take place next week between Israeli Prime Minister Ehud Olment, U.S. Secretary of State Condoleezza Rice, and Palestinian President Abbas. I submit that the issue of *root causes* of the conflicts in the Middle East must be addressed and satisfactorily resolved in order for a genuine peace process to begin. In order for this to happen, peacemakers are needed.

Where are the peacemakers?

CHAPTER 21

Meetings in Jerusalem—February 21, 2007

This week, for the first time, U.S. Secretary of State Condoleezza Rice, Palestinian Authority President Mahmud Abbas, and Israeli Prime Minister Ehud Olmet met. The meeting, which brought the United States, Palestinians, and Israelis together, was the first of its kind since the 2000 Camp David Retreat in the United States during President Bill Clinton's administration—was held in Jerusalem to discuss the ongoing Palestinian-Israeli conflict and prospects for "peace." The meeting came after Palestinians met in Mecca, Saudi Arabia, and reached a tentative agreement to form a government of national unity (the sharing of political and economic power between Hamas and Fatah, a way forward for the Palestinian people). Since Mecca, Palestinians—Fatah and Hamas—met and continued to work on the specifics of a proposed 'unity government.' As a follow-up to the meeting in Mecca—and in an agreement—Palestinian Prime Minister Ismail Heniyeh resigned. As part of the resignation and agreement, Heniyeh is now tasked with spearheading efforts to form a Palestinian government of national unit. As these dynamics were unfolding, attention began to focus on Jerusalem.

During the weekend prior to the recent meeting, separate meetings were held with Secretary of State Rice, President Abbas, and Prime Minister Olmet. There were clear expressions from Secretary of State Rice that under any agreements between Fatah and Hamas, the Middle East Quartet's "principles" must be observed (the U.S., United Nations, Russia, and the European Union). What are those "principles?" Hamas must: 1) recognize Israel's 'right to exist', 2) renounce violence, and 3) accept past Israeli-Palestinian agreements and accords.

The much anticipated meeting of the three was held in Jerusalem on Monday, February 19, 2007; President Abbas presented and defended information and views about the recent agreement between the Palestinian Authority (Fatah) and Hamas to form a government of national unity. Secretary Rice and Israeli Prime Minister Olmet acknowledged the agreement between the Palestinian Authority and Hamas—while at the same time expressing reservations and concerns. Secretary Rice stated that the Quartet's "principles" are the basis for reservations and concerns.

Something is missing. Major Arab concerns and issues—*root causes*—are not raised or addressed in the Quartet's "principles." Some of the issues are Arab land (1948, before and now), Israeli military occupation of Arab land (the land is referred to by the 'international community' as "occupied territory"), Palestinians killed by members of the Israeli Defense Force, treatment of Palestinians during the past 59 years—since 1948 (refugees, the internally displaced, those held in Israeli jails), and the fact that Arab countries and other European countries are also part of the "international community." Facts are very important. They should not be hidden, dismissed, ignored, or distorted. The honest thing to do is face up to the facts and work to find peaceful solutions.

Fundamental and major issues underlining the ongoing conflict between the Israelis and the Palestinians were not part of the "peace discussions" in Jerusalem. Very little—if anything—was accomplished. Following the meeting, Secretary of State Rice announced that they all agreed to meet again. Hopefully, the *root causes* of the conflict will be acknowledged at some point by those who continue to meet—all over the world. There is no time better than the present to do so.

Where are the peacemakers?

CHAPTER 22

Iraq: What Have We Learned?— February 27, 2007

Next month will mark the fourth year since the U.S.-led invasion of Iraq. What have we learned? It has become very clear that certain issues and facts have been brought to the public's attention. The issues and facts have provided a basis for concerned individuals to become better informed—and more engaged—especially from a factually informed position.

1. In March 2003, the U.S. invaded Iraq as the American people were told that Iraq was manufacturing and stockpiling weapons of mass destruction (WMD). The American people—and other people of the world—were told that there were various countries supporting the invasion ("coalition of the willing").

2. Two months after the invasion, in May 2003, President George W. Bush publicly declared to America and the world—"mission accomplished." Whatever the "mission" was or is, it was not accomplished by May 2003 or by February 2007.

3. Four years later, thousands of lives have been lost, thousands have been wounded, and become internally displaced, thousands have become refugees, and thousands continue to face violence and the threat of violence daily.

4. Iraq's infrastructure has been severely damaged. There is a lack of power and water in many parts of the country—including Baghdad, the capital city.

5. In the face of opposition from the U.S. Congress and the American people, President Bush has maintained that America will not "cut and run," America will "stay the course."

6. On January 10, 2007, President Bush announced a "surge"—21,500 more American troops will be sent to Iraq.

7. On February 21, 2007, British Prime Minister Tony Blair, the U.S.'s closest partner in the "coalition of the willing," announced to the British House of Commons that Britain will begin a phase withdrawal of its remaining 7,100 troops from Iraq—1,500 troops in the next few months and one half by the end of the year. Three years ago, Britain had 40,000 troops in Iraq.

8. The anticipated announcement by Prime Minister Blair led President Bush to state that Blair's statement was a "sign of success."

Currently, the U.S. is supplying 91% of the foreign troops in combat in Iraq, Britain 5%, and a few other countries a combined 4%. Several other countries have withdrawn troops and other countries never committed any troops. The 91%, the 5%, and the 4% should not be in Iraq. Some countries realized that their troops were in the wrong country, and some countries did not make the error in judgment and send troops in the first place.

No weapons of mass destruction have been found.

Chapter 23

Problems and Solutions—March 4, 2007

During the past weeks, Iraq, Iran, The Quarter on the Middle East peace process, and China featured at some point in the major news highlights. On Wednesday, February 21, 2007, The Quartet: the United Nations, United States, European Union, and Russia, met in Berlin, Germany.

The meeting was a follow-up to the meeting in Washington, D.C. on Friday, February 2, 2007. Around the same time, UN Secretary General Ban Ki Moon dispatched a UN Envoy, Special Representative to Iran, Ashraf Qazi as part of ongoing efforts to focus on the violent and bloody conflict in Iraq. Qazi's mission was to engage Iraqi officials in a dialogue centered on supporting constructive efforts to bring the conflict in Iraq to an end. In other words, the UN is playing a major role regarding Iraq and Iran. It is worth pointing out here that it was this same UN that told the world in 2002 and since, that their inspectors did not find any weapons of mass destruction in Iraq. It is the same UN that called on the United States to provide evidence of weapons of mass destruction and did not give support to the proposed U.S.-led invasion of Iraq in 2003. The Quartet recognizes parts of the problems that exist (symptoms), but the Quartet is not seizing the opportunities to address fundamental issues regarding Iraq (causes) and to help bring forth peaceful solutions.

As the Quartet was meeting in Berlin, U.S. Vice President Dick Chaney was in Tokyo, Japan, talking about the U.S. leaving Iraq "with honor." During his visit, he took the opportunity to blast Democrats in the U.S. Senate for challenging President George Bush and his plans for Iraq (strategy and troop build-up). He was silent to the fact that there are Republicans as well who are raising questions, issues, and objections (including votes) in the U.S. House of Representatives and the U.S. Senate. After Japan, Vice President Chaney traveled to Australia. While in Sydney, he took the opportunity—and the liberty—to praise China for being instrumental in negotiations with North Korea regarding concerns about North Korea's admitted nuclear program. He criticized China for what he refers to as China's 'rapid military build-up.' Vice President Chaney stated that China was "not consistent" with its own stated aims to curtail the global arms race. There were no issues raised publicly about China's human rights record.

The meetings with 'key stakeholders' are designed to address problems and conflicts around the world (the Quarter is also supposed to help resolve the decades old conflict between the Palestinians and the Israelis, the Israelis and the Lebanese, and more). The 'key stakeholders' are aware—or should be aware of—the consequences of prolonged and protracted unsettled conflicts.

Unfortunately, they are discussing the symptoms—not the causes. There is a better way out of this violent madness. The world is being led towards World War III, violence, war, and insecurity (more violence, more wars, and more insecurity).

The multi-billion-dollar arms industry—manufacturing and distributing of arms—is the major contributor to war, violence, insecurity, and instability in the world today. Given this situation, what is the solution? I prescribe that **all** weapons of human destruction be destroyed. Can this be done practically today, tomorrow, next week, or next month? The answer is no. Can a commitment be made by the manufacturers and distributors of arms to halt plans, manufacturing and distributing of arms today, tomorrow, next week, or next month? The answer is yes.

What is morally correct about any nation or nations saying to another nation or nations—you cannot and should not have such weapons—especially when the nation and nations making the demands have huge stockpiles of weapons—perhaps enough to blow up the world ten times over? Ironically, 49 nations met just recently in Oslo, Norway. One of the key items on the agenda was cluster bombs (large number of bomblets packed into artillery shells). Forty-six (46) of the 49 nations voted for a proposed global treaty to ban cluster bombs. The three leading large arms manufacturing and distributing nations in the world did not participate in the meeting: the United States, China, and Russia. The three nations opposing the proposed ban were Japan, Poland, and Romania. Japan is one of the leading nations which manufactures and distributes small arms. The United States and Israel are among 14 countries that have established small arms and ammunition licensed production with 45 countries. Israel did not participate in the Oslo meeting.

Several years ago, more than 100 nations voted for a proposal to ban landmines. Landmines are responsible for killing and wounding thousands of people worldwide—mostly civilians (World War I, World War II, the Korean War, the Vietnam War, the Gulf War, the Balkans War, the Iraq War, and other wars and conflicts). In spite of this gloomy reality, there were nations that voted to oppose the banning of landmines. Some of these very same nations were still dancing to the tune of financial profits and war when they voted against a proposed treaty to ban cluster bombs. The ultimate security of the world is linked to love, justice, and peace—not weapons and war. "Wisdom is better than weapons of war" (Ecclesiastes 9:18).

Where are the peacemakers?

CHAPTER 24

Iraq: Another Meeting, New Signals—
March 6, 2007

Last week, U.S. Secretary of State Condoleezza Rice announced that the U.S. is launching new talks 'to secure Iraq.' In making the important announcement, she stated, "I am pleased to announce that we are supporting the Iraqis in a new diplomatic offensive, to build greater support, both within the region and beyond, for peace and prosperity in Iraq." She stated, 'We hope that all governments seize this opportunity to improve their relations with Iraq and to work for peace and stability in the region.' Secretary Rice pointed out that Iraqis and U.S. officials agree that progress and success in Iraq "require the positive support of Iraq's neighbors." This language represents 'new signals' in the deadly and bloody four year old conflict in Iraq. It suggests that Iran, Syria, and other neighboring countries will be recognized and openly invited to participate in a meeting—perhaps as soon as next week. In addition to neighboring countries, all members of the United Nations (UN) Security Council will be invited and encouraged to participate in the meeting: the United States, Britain, France, Russia, and China.

Given these 'new signals,' the indications are suggesting that the arena for dialogue is being expanded. This is a positive sign. Expanding the arena for dialogue is what many have been calling for all along, including *The Iraq Study Group Report: The Way Forward—A New Approach* (2006). Expanding the arena for dialogue is necessary. Equally important, fundamental issues and concerns by all key stakeholders—especially those countries in the region—must be genuinely recognized by all participants. When and if there is genuine recognition, the meeting and future meetings will have some realistic chances of making real differences in Iraq, Iran, Lebanon, and other situations and countries where there are conflicts and potential conflicts. It is my hope that this will be the case. Lives, stability, and security are at stake.

There is a need for peacemakers to step forward.

CHAPTER 25

Darfur: A United Nations Report—
March 21, 2007

On Monday, March 12, 2007, the United Nations Human Rights Council issued a report concerning the four-year-old violent, bloody and deadly conflict in Darfur, Sudan—Africa. The report clearly stated that 1) the government of Sudan has failed to protect the people in Darfur from attacks by the Janjaweed faction and 2) the government of Sudan has participated in the crimes which have been and are being committed in Darfur.

Some of what was stated in the report is relatively new. Most of what was stated in the report is well known by the people in Darfur and Sudan, on the African Continent, and broader population (especially leaders) throughout the world. At the same time, Sudan government officials have denied any knowledge or involvement concerning the Janjaweed—the faction that is responsible for rape, torture, and murder in Darfur. Prior to the UN report's release, the International Criminal Court (ICC) in The Hague, Netherlands, issued statements linking the government of Sudan to the Janjaweed and atrocities in Darfur.

Although it is encouraging to see the United Nations report being released and to know that Darfur is on the radar at the United Nations—and stronger intervention, sanctions, and criminal prosecution are being recommended, swift and immediate action is needed now. The UN Security Council can make a difference. The question is, will the Council step forth and make a difference? Adding to this challenge is the fact that two Council members are directly engaged in Darfur and Sudan for economic and political reasons. China is directly engaged in Darfur because of its oil interests (Darfur is rich in oil). Russia is directly engaged in Sudan and Darfur because of arms sales and financial benefits from the arms sales. Darfur and the United Nations report is a familiar scenario. The causes are clearly identified. The report will be discussed at the UN and around the world. The fundamental question is, what—if anything—will be done? In order to address and resolve the Darfur conflict, more than talk is needed. The opportunities are there to do something. Will it happen? Hopefully, it will.

The violent, bloody, and deadly conflict should come to an end. Since 2003, more than 225,000 people have been killed, and close to 3 million people have been displaced.

Peace is needed.

Save the people of Darfur!

Where are the peacemakers?

Chapter 26

Easter Sunday, April 8, 2007: Pope Benedict XVI's Message—April 12, 2007

On Easter Sunday, April 8, 2007, Pope Benedict XVI delivered the annual message from St. Peter's Square at the Vatican. The Pope took the opportunity during his message to acknowledge the resurrection of Jesus Christ—'the Prince of Peace.' The Pope spoke about violence, bloodshed, and death around the world and the "continued slaughter" in Iraq, the conflict in Afghanistan, and conflicts in specific countries.

In his message, which he addressed to "Brothers and Sisters throughout the world, men and women of good will," he stated, "Christ is risen! Peace to you! Today we celebrate the great mystery, the foundation of Christian faith and hope: Jesus of Nazareth, the crucified one, has risen from the dead on the third day according to the Scriptures." The Pope spoke to the descriptive and significant history of the death and the resurrection of Jesus Christ (Luke 24:5-6, John 12:26, 20:19, and 20:27-28, and 1st Peter 2:24).

On this Easter Sunday, the Pope commented about the ongoing Middle East conflict between Israel and the Palestinians. Africa was on the Pope's radar as well. He spoke about the humanitarian situation that has been created by men in Darfur, Sudan. He spoke about the violent situations in Somalia, and the Democratic Republic of the Congo. Perhaps in efforts to prevent yet another such situation from developing into a full-scale outbreak, he spoke about the tense and sometimes violent situation in Zimbabwe.

As the Pope addressed his message to "Brothers and Sisters throughout the world, men and women of good will," we should asked ourselves—was he talking to us? If so, what will we continue to do for peace? If we feel the Pope was not speaking to us, we should ask ourselves why? Are we brothers or sisters to someone in this world? Are we persons of good will? As children of God, we must say and do something.

Where are the peacemakers?

CHAPTER 27

Continued Fighting and Bloodshed in the Middle East—June 25, 2007

"We have limited options, and most of them are bad."

—Martin S. Indyk
former U.S. Ambassador to Israel
June 13, 2007

The ongoing fighting and bloodshed in the Middle East continues—with no realistic end in sight. There are more fighting, deaths, bloodshed, refugees, and people being internally displaced. Martin Indyk, former U.S. Ambassador to Israel, raised a valid point that is shared by many when he stated, "We have limited options, and most of them are bad." Writing in *The Guardian* newspaper, Michael Boyle called it, "The Fruits of Neglect." Boyle states, "The violence in Gaza is the results of the Bush administration's half-hearted policy towards the Israel-Palestinian dispute" (www.Guardian.co.uk/commentisfree).

Recently, intense fighting between Hamas and Fatah resulted with Humas gaining control of Gaza. In response, Israel, the United States, and the European Union (EU) voiced their continued support [financial and political] for Palestinian President Mahmoud Abbas. Instead of these stakeholders working to help bring Hamas and Fatah closer together for an *internal peace*—they continue to use the strategy of 'divide and conquer' (and rule)—failing to realize the consequences—a continuing delay of an *external peace* (peace between Israel and the Palestinians).

Former U.S. President Jimmy Carter, speaking to the Annual Forum on Human Rights in Dublin, Ireland, stated that the United States, Israel, and the European Union's latest voiced support for Abbas' government in the West Bank is an "effort to divide Palestinians into two people." President Carter's analysis is correct (for more background, see Carter's book, *Palestine: Peace Not Apartheid*, 2006).

Reflecting on Ambassador Indyk's comment about "limited options," I wonder if President Bush and Israel Prime Minister Ehud Olmert listened, heard, or understood. Recent news out of Washington is that President Bush has spoken to British Prime Minister Tony Blair about becoming a Middle East Envoy after he steps down as Prime Minister soon. News out of Israel is that Prime Minister Olmert has indicated support for such an idea. What has Prime Minister Blair done for peace in the Middle East? If such an idea moves forward, it will clearly be one of the 'bad limited options.'

Where are the peacemakers?

CHAPTER 28

Critical Issues—September 25, 2007

Once again, the Israeli and Palestinian conflict re-surfaced high on the media agenda this past week. On Wednesday, September 19, 2007, U.S. Secretary of State Condoleezza Rice traveled to the Middle East for the purpose of meeting with high ranking government officials of Israel and the Palestinian Authority—concerning the conflict and a proposed U.S. peace conference to address what she calls "critical issues." As the on again, off again, and seemingly unending "peace" discussions continue—Secretary Rice was quoted in Shannon, Ireland, as saying, "Nobody wants to have a meeting where people simply come and sit and talk and talk and talk." During a brief stop-over in route, she emphasized that "critical issues" will be addressed in an upcoming U.S.-led "peace conference" on the Middle East. Speaking about the prospects of a "peace conference," Secretary Rice said, "Everyone expects to be serious and substantive, and everybody expects it to address critical issues."

In July of this year, in a bold and pronounced challenge, Secretary Rice correctly called for "root causes" of the conflict to be addressed (see #2, Where Are the Peacemakers? "Israel and the Palestinians," July 26, 2007). Whether it is "root causes" or "critical issues"—there is a need to move beyond the rhetoric and meetings, face up to certain truths and realities, and come forth with concrete prescriptions and solutions. I agree with the sentiments of Secretary Rice's voiced concerns. Unfortunately, meetings and more meetings—talk and more talk—will not necessarily resolve the conflict. I submit that in order for security, peace, stability, and justice to prevail—honest, sincere, substantive, and consistent action is needed. Peacemakers will insure that certain factual realities are placed at the heart and center of the discourse. In other words, move beyond 'the state of denial' and address realities. Peacemakers will honestly address the fundamental issues—"root causes" and or "critical issues." What are the "root causes"? What are the "critical issues?" The historical and contemporary realities are related to land in general, Jerusalem in particular, refugees, settlements that exist and are built and expanded, a concrete wall that is being built by Israel, and thousands of Palestinians being held as prisoners in Israeli jails. At some point, sooner or later, these realities—"root causes" or "critical issues"—must be adequately addressed.

Where are the peacemakers?

CHAPTER 29

'Elders' Pursue Peace in Sudan—
October 26, 2007

A number of highly recognized and well-respected statespersons have joined the efforts to bring about a just and peaceful resolution to the violent, bloody, and deadly conflict in Sudan. After years of bloodshed, destruction, deaths, and injured and or displaced people, 'elder' statespersons from outside Sudan have stepped into the conflict—in efforts to help bring about a just and peaceful solution. The 'elders' effort is being led by Nelson Mandela, Desmond Tutu, Jimmy Carter, Graca Machel, and others.

To date, efforts have been made to bring about a 'political solution' to the conflict in Sudan. The 'elders,' working from a 'non-political' position, brings about a different approach to the process. There is a paradigm shift. According to David Monyal, a history professor at Witswaterand University in Johannesburg, South Africa, "there is no doubt that the role of elders has been a part of African politics . . . they bring a continuity and experience and a credibility that, especially in a conflict-torn country, would be a good use and quite welcome."

CHAPTER 30

Youth and Youth Leaders Pursue Peace: Israel and the Palestinians—November 3, 2007

Palestinian and Israeli youth and youth leaders are weighing in on the ongoing conflict between Israel and the Palestinians. Working through a combination of organizations—Onevoice Peace Movement and The Peaceworks Foundation—Israeli and Palestinian youth and youth leaders are working together, calling on each other (and representatives) to work together and bring about a peaceful resolution to the violent, bloody, and deadly conflict.

According to its statement, since 2002, "Onevoice has undertaken a grassroots approach to engage Palestinians and Israelis towards greater civic involvement . . . Onevoice Movement has striven to empower the moderate majority of Israelis and Palestinians to take a more active, assertive role toward resolving the conflict." Onevoice developed a number of activities which are designed to help meet its objectives. Included among those activities are Leadership Development Workshops, Mobilization Training Seminars, Regional College Tours, and an International Education Program. Through these and other activities, efforts are being made to *inform, educate,* and *engage.* Through these various channels and others, efforts are being made to pursue peace. Youth and youth leaders—Israeli and Palestinians—working with each other at home and abroad—are trying to find ways to end the conflict.

You can read about these activities and organizations (see http://www.onevoice.com, http://www.onemillionvoices.org, and http://www.onevoicemovement.org). After reading about 'Onevoice' and "Onevoice Movement for Peace'—then discussing the activities and organizations with others, there is something else you can do. IF you agree with what these organizations stand for—you can get more involved. You can do so by lending your support, joining, encouraging others to join, making financial contributions and encouraging others to do the same, distributing information to others within your network, and more. Informed, engaged, and actively participating—you can help make a positive difference. You can help answer the question.

Where are the peacemakers?

CHAPTER 31

Pope Benedict XVI's Christmas Message: An Appeal to Political Leaders— December 26, 2007

Pope Benedict XVI, speaking from the balcony at St. Peter's Basilica in the Vatican City on Tuesday, December 25, 2007, issued his annual Christmas message. Pope Benedict, first recognized the birth of Jesus Christ and the important meaning of Jesus' birth and existence to all of humankind. Later, he appealed to political leaders of the world to muster "wisdom and courage" and bring an end to the bloody wars and conflicts around the globe.

In a message of peace and hope, which was translated into 63 different languages, the Pope spoke of the victims—especially children and the elderly—called on leaders to seek "humane, just, and lasting solutions" to wars and conflicts in the world. He specifically mentioned wars and bloodshed in Darfur (Sudan), Somalia, Afghanistan, Iraq, Congo, Israel and the Palestinians, Pakistan, Lebanon, Eritrea, Ethiopia, Sri Lanka, and the Balkans.

As many people in different parts of the world celebrated Christ's birthday, the Pope (and a few other religious leaders) took advantage of an opportunity to speak out once again about wars around the world. His message was timely and important. It was timely because the world's attention—for one day—was focused in part on a savior, Jesus Christ. It was important because the wars and bloodshed are bringing about the opposite of that which Jesus Christ came to do—direct men and women to God, advance peace, love, justice, and brotherhood, heal the sick, feed the hungry, and clothe the naked.

Hopefully, the Pope's message will not fall on deaf ears. The political leaders have ears to hear and eyes to see. Will they hear and see?

Where are the peacemakers?

THE FINAL ANALYSIS

In the Final Analysis, peacemakers are needed. Peacekeepers, however well intended, will not substitute for peacemakers. Why is this so? The response is very simple. The first step is to make the peace; the peace has not been made. Peace which has not been made cannot be kept. Currently, there is a 17,000-member "United Nations Peacekeeping Force" in the Congo, Africa (MONUC), the largest 'peacekeeping force' in the world. In a published newspaper articled titled, "Peacekeepers without a peace to keep," the *New York Times* stated it very clearly (Sunday, October 14, 2007, p. 5). We must be factually accurate and logically consistent in what we say and do. We must tell the truth—the whole truth. With very few exceptions, this is not being done.

There is a better way. We must respect the spiritual and moral accords of nature. We must be grounded and guided by love, justice, and truth. We must respect one another as individuals, communities, territories, and nations. We must pursue peace—not just seek peace. If we sincerely do all of these things, the peace will come.

APPENDIX—MAPS

Iraq

Israel

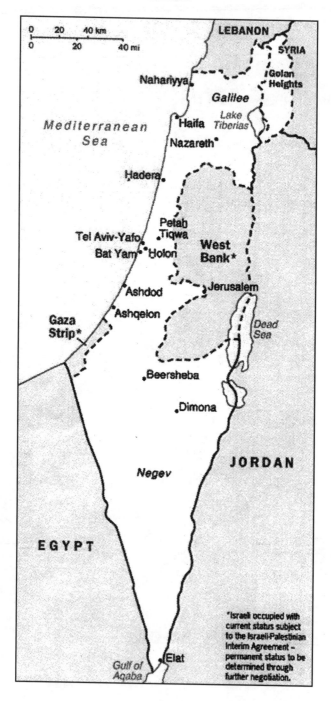

Lebanon

Republic of Serpska

Afghanistan

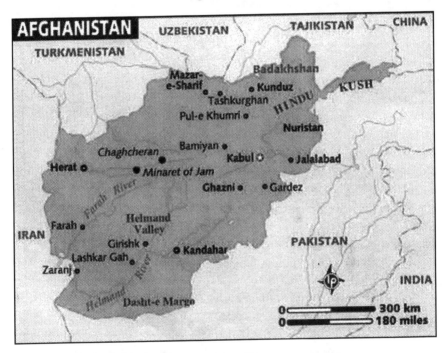

Uganda

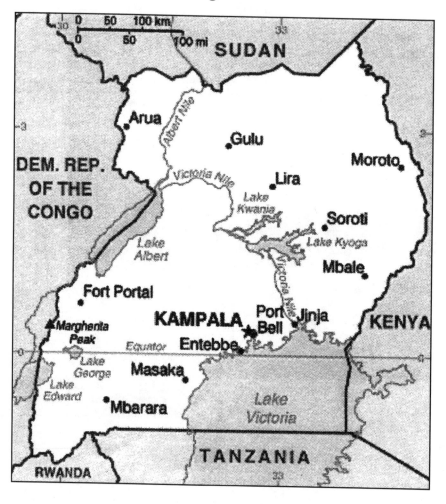

Selected References

A. Songs

B. Books

C. Newspapers and Magazines

D. Organizations

E. Documents

F. Reports

A. Songs

"We are the World"—Michael Jackson and Lionel Ritchie

"Wake Up Everybody"—Harold Melvin and the Blue Notes

"How To Dismantle An Atomic Bomb"—U2

"Imagine"—John Lennon

"What a Friend We Have in Jesus"—Joseph M. Scriven

"Ain't Gonna Study War No More"

"A Charge To Keep"—Charles Wesley

"Stand By Me"—Ben E. King

"Precious Lord Take My Hand"—Tommy Dorsey

"From A Distance"—Bette Midler

"Steal Away"—Wallis Willis

"Blind Men"—Rev. James Cleveland

"Georgia On My Mind"—Ray Charles

"Jesus Is The Best Thing That Ever Happened To Me"—Rev. James Cleveland

"War"—Edwin Starr

B. Books

African Methodist Episcopal Church 1994-1995 Yearbook

Bush At War by Bob Woodward

Democracy Matters by Cornell West

Does America Need A Foreign Policy? Towards a Diplomacy for the Twenty First Century by Henry Kissinger

God Has A Dream: A Vision of Hope for our Times by Desmond Tutu

Heroes and Saracens by Norman Daniel

Holy Bible

Palestine: Peace Not Apartheid by Jimmy Carter

Political Thinking by Glenn Tinder

State of Denial by Bob Woodward

The State of America's Children by Children's Defense Fund

Tyranny of the Majority: Fundamental Fairness in Political Representation by Lani Guinier

Where Do We Go From Here: Chaos or Community? by Rev. Dr. Martin Luther King, Jr.

Wounded Childhood

C. Newspapers and Magazines

NEWSPAPERS

The International Herald Tribune

The New Vision

The Daily Monitor

The Final Call

The Sowetan

The Daily Mirror

The Guardian

The New York Times

The Washington Post

The East African

The Los Angeles Times

The Wall Street Journal

The Baltimore Sun

MAGAZINES

The Economist

D. Organizations

The United Nations (UN)

The Children's Defense Fund

The African Methodist Episcopal Church

Women's Missionary Society

Stockholm International Research Institute

Lord's Resistance Army (LRA)

Centre for Nonproliferation Studies

Monterey Institute of International Studies

The African Centre on the Rights and Welfare of the Child (ARCWC)

The United Nations Commission on Human Rights (UNHCR)

The United Nations World Health Organization (WHO)

The Regional African Juvenile Justice Network

The United Nations Children Education Fund (UNICEF)

The United Nations Security Council

African Women for Peace

The African Union (AU)

Women Building Peace

South Africa's Truth and Reconciliation Commission

Women Waging Peace

United Nations Development Fund for Women

Israeli Defense Force (IDF)

The American Academy of Arts and Sciences

New America Foundation

Palestine Liberation Organization (PLO)

One Voice

One Voice Movement for Peace

E. Documents

Letter from a Birmingham Jail, April 16, 1963

The Balfour Declaration, 1917

Education, BC

Small Arms Survey, 2001

The Beautiful Children, 1994-1995

"Making Children Count"—The UN Study on Violence Against Children, 2004

United Nations Resolution 1559

United Nations Resolution 1680

United Nations Resolution 1701

United Nations Resolution 194

United Nations Resolution 242

United Nations Resolution 338

F. Reports

The State of America's Children by the Children's Defense Fund

About the Author

During the past three decades, Jerry Henderson has lived and worked in twenty (20) countries, including eleven (11) war and conflict zones, engaged providing technical assistance and capacity building support in the areas of democracy, governance, elections, legislative strengthening, and conflict mitigation. He has worked in local, state and national government in the United States, and has consulted for international development, peace building and humanitarian organizations, including the United Nations (UN), the Organization for Security and Cooperation in Europe (OSCE), the Africa-American Institute (AAI), the International Foundation for Electoral Systems (IFES), the National Democratic Institute for International Affairs (NDI), Development Associates, and Research Triangle Institute International (RTI).

Jerry was born in Troy, Alabama. He is a graduate of the Troy City Public School System. In addition to doing post graduate studies, he is a graduate of Atlanta University—now Clark Atlanta University, Atlanta, Georgia—MA degree in political science and Brooklyn College, Brooklyn, New York, BA degree in political science.

He has served as Director of Elections for the state of Alabama, Office of the Secretary of State, member of state Advisory Board for Voter Registration, a founding member of the National Association of State Election Directors (NASED), an elected public official, an adjunct instructor of government and political science, a special guest lecturer at universities in the United States as well as in Guyana, Zambia, Kenya, and Uganda. He has spoken at primary and secondary schools and one kindergarten class.

Jerry is a community volunteer, a Life member of Rotary International (Paul Harris Fellow), Deborah Hospital Foundation, and the National Association for the Advancement of Colored People (NAACP). He is a member of the Academy of Political Science, National Association of Black County Officials (NABCO), Black Professionals in International Affairs (BPIA), and a Wilson Center Associate.

INDEX

D

Da Costa, Paulinho 45
Daily Mirror, The 5
Daily Monitor, The 61, 121
Damascus 6-7
Daniel, Norman 32, 34, 120
Darfur 62, 67-8, 97-9, 109
Davis, Merryl Wyn 80
deaths 14-15, 21, 26, 47-9, 82, 101, 105
December 67, 71, 74, 109
defense 23, 47, 53, 81, 88, 121-4
Democratic Republic of the Congo
    3, 49, 99
demonstrations 6-8, 81
Denmark 6
Denver 6
description 39
destruction v, 4-5, 7, 14, 17-19,
    21-3, 26-7, 31, 34, 39-41, 54-5,
    67, 75, 77, 89-92
diamonds 14
diplomacy 10, 26-7, 80, 120
Dorsey, Tommy 120
drawing 24, 67, 75
DRC 3, 49
Dublin 7, 101

E

Earth Summit 2, 34
East African, The 5, 121
East Timor 3
Easter Sunday 99
Ecclesiastes 18, 26, 93
Economist, The 5
economy 35
Edelman, Marian Wright 47-8, 54
educate 32, 61, 107
education 31-3, 35, 49-51, 60, 67-8,
    79, 107, 122-3
Eisenhower, Dwight David 40
El Salvador 3

Elders 105
elections 35, 85-6, 125
Emerson, Ralph Waldo 32-3
encourage 35
encouragement 18
Envoy 91, 102
Eritrea 3, 49, 77, 109
Ethiopia 3, 49, 68, 77, 109
EU 68, 83, 101
European Union 68, 83, 87, 91, 101
Exodus 36
experts 33
extremists 32

F

Faith 47, 99
Father 64
Final Call, The 5
Florida 48
Former Soviet Union (Russia) 3
France 7, 21, 27, 41, 49, 68, 95
Friend 5, 14-15, 36, 42, 57, 119

G

G8 4
Gates, Robert M. 81
Gaza Strip 9, 85
Geldolf, Bob 45
Generic peace 14
Geneva 41
Genocide 67
Georgia 46, 120, 125
Germany 6-7, 41, 84, 91
Ghandi, Mahatma 29, 34
Gibson, Fanta 64
Gift 55
God vi, 7-8, 18, 23, 34, 36, 39, 42,
    45-6, 55, 65, 74, 100, 109, 120
Golan Heights 22
Graham, Rev. Billy 74
Grammy 45

New America Foundation 27, 123
New Vision 60-1, 121
New York 5, 7, 15, 48, 75, 111, 121, 125
New York Amsterdam News 5
New York Times 5, 111, 121
Nigeria 2, 49, 77
night commuters 61
Nobel Prize for Peace 1
Norway 92

O

Ohio 46
Oil 14, 71, 97
Olment, Ehud 86
Omartian, Michael 45
Omega Foundation 41
One Dream 60
oppression 39
Oprah 61-2
Oprah Winfrey Show 61
organizations 7, 9, 24, 31-2, 35, 37,
    40, 55, 68, 85, 107, 119, 122
Osborne, Jeffrey 45
Oslo 10, 92-3
Oslo Agreement 10
Oxford Research Group 6

P

PAHEHO ALETHHCTBO 56
pain 5, 8, 15, 26, 36
Pakistan 2, 6, 109
Palestinian Authority 85, 87-8, 103
Palestinian Liberation Organization
    28, 85, 123
Palestinian Territory 9, 24, 77-8
Palestinians 9, 23, 83-5, 87-8, 92,
    99, 101-4, 107, 109
Panama 2
Parks, Rosa 32
Parliament 46, 85
passed 21, 23, 25

Payne, Freda 42
Peacekeeping 1-2, 10-11, 21, 27, 111
Pennsylvania 7, 75
Per capita 49-50
Peres, Shimeon 2
Peru 7
Peter 99, 109
Philadelphia 7, 46, 48
Philippines 2
Phillinganes, Greg 45
PLO 85-6, 123
poetry 55, 61, 64
Pointer Sisters 45
Poland 92
police district 48
pontificate 5, 13-14
Portugal 41
Poverty v, 43, 47, 49, 55, 67, 77
power 3, 14, 24-5, 34, 40, 85, 87, 89
pragmatic 27, 35
prescription 15, 24, 34-5, 39-40
Pretoria 53
Prime Minister 9-10, 85-8, 90, 102
Promised Land 34
Prophets 19
Psalms 26
Puerto Rico 7
pursue 26, 80, 105, 107, 111

Q

Qatar 22
Qazi, Ashraf 91
Quartet 83-4, 87-8, 91
Quick-fix solutions 14
Quicksand 76

R

Raleigh 7
Ramsey, Charles H. 48
raped 67
real peace 14

rebels 32, 60-1

Regional Africa Juvenile Justice
Network 51, 68, 122

Regional College Tours 107

Republika Serpska 55

resolution 15, 17, 21-3, 25-7, 84,
105, 107, 124

Rice, Condoleezza 9, 13, 86-7, 95, 103

Richie, Lionel 45

Rights and Welfare 53, 68, 122

Road map to Peace 83

Robinson, Smokey 45

rocket 13, 40

Roger, Kenny 45

Rogue state 32

Romania 92

Rome 6-7, 13

root causes 9-10, 13-15, 21-5, 27-8,
83, 85-6, 88, 103-4

Ross, Diana 45

Rowan, William 22

Russia 3, 6, 41, 68, 83, 87, 91-2,
95, 97

Rwanda 2, 49, 67

S

San Diego 7

San Francisco 6-7

Saudi Arabia 41, 78, 85, 87

Scriptures 8, 26, 36, 99

Scriven, Joseph M 119

Secretary General 2, 10, 13, 19, 22,
68-9, 71, 91

security 7-8, 10, 14-15, 18, 21-2,
25, 27, 40, 74, 77-80, 84, 93,
95, 97, 103

Security Council 21-2, 25, 95, 97, 122

Senate Foreign Relations
Committee 81

Senegal 7

Sentamu, John 22

settlements 104

Shannon 103

Shebba Farms 21

Sierra Leone 2, 49

Sinful 8, 15, 26

Singapore 41

sinners 65

slavery 67

Sleep 61

Small Arms Reduction
Programme 41

Small Arms Survey 41, 123

smart bombs 36

Smyhtes, Steven 60

Socrates 32-3

Somalia 2, 49, 99, 109

Song 5, 15, 42, 45

Sound of Philadelphia 46

South Africa 1-3, 7, 18-19, 34, 41,
53, 105, 123

South Africa Truth and Reconciliation
Commission 1, 123

South Carolina 46

sovereignty 14

Sowetan, The 5, 121

Spain 7

Springsteen, Bruce 45

Sri Lanka 3, 109

St. Peter's Basilica 109

St. Peter's Square 99

Starks, Jessie 46

Starr, Edwin 46, 120

State of America's Children 53, 121, 124

Stockholm International Research
Institute 122

strategic 4, 14

Sudan 3, 49, 62, 67-9, 77, 97, 99,
105, 109

suffering 5, 13, 15, 19, 26, 62

Sunday 99, 111

Switzerland 7, 41

Sydney 7, 92

Syria 6-7, 26, 28, 78, 95